MUSICAL INSTRUMENTS
made to be played

Plate 1. A pattern of instruments. In addition to showing many of the instruments described in the book, this photograph shows the frame and soundboard assembly of a Spinet and also a Fidel with its bow. Nearby lies the template for a viola back.

MUSICAL INSTRUMENTS
made to be played

RONALD ROBERTS

Principal Lecturer in Craftwork, Saint Luke's College, Exeter

THE DRYAD PRESS

Fourth Edition, Revised, 1969

Published by the Dryad Press, Leicester
and printed in **Great Britain** *by* **The Blackfriars Press Ltd.,** *Leicester*

Contents

Acknowledgments

IN preparing the material for this book I have become indebted to, and wish to thank:

Miss Winsome Bartlett for her advice on tacked drums; Miss Margaret Galloway for permission to include some of her work on rubber drums and the tubular glockenspiel; Mr. John Hosier for the idea of the "lagerphone"; Miss Doreen Senior for her encouragement over a long period; Professor Edgar Stahmer for the details of the bowed psaltery and the basis of the resonated xylophone; Miss Mabel Wilson for suggestions about simple percussion; the Principal and members of the staff of Saint Luke's College for the facilities and encouragement I have enjoyed from the beginning of this work.

R. R.

Foreword

THIS book is written from the conviction—borne out by experience with groups of children and adults—that the making and use of a musical instrument, in sequence, are activities which need not be reserved entirely for highly-skilled people. Musical sound-producers may be made at all ages between early primary years and maturity. Children of pre-school years are already interested in any device which will make sounds, and those who are given early in school life the chance to collect and assemble simple musical devices will be keen to make and play more intricate ones later. They become involved to the extent that satisfaction can be achieved only by further experiment. This state of involvement is usually accompanied by a strong impulse to learn. The instruments become very personal possessions and I have heard of children who have refused to be parted from their instruments on leaving the primary school. This is not surprising. Musical instruments have always been treasured from early times; they have often been richly and lovingly embellished, as we can see from many examples in museums.

The work presented should lead in many ways to activities which individual teachers may be able to enlarge. Young people find this experimental work with materials absorbing and rewarding. Much present-day teaching of art and craft is based on the creative use of the materials available and on knowledge of their texture and colour. Further knowledge of the acoustic values of materials may be related to what is already known of their other physical characteristics. The visual appeal of much of the material described is valuable and this reinforces the appeal of the sounds produced. In fact, with young children, the visual appeal is often the stronger.

It is sometimes forgotten that the intense interest aroused by a class activity in craft may have a profound influence upon vocabulary, both spoken and written. New words and expressions are used freely in context and there is often visual and tactile evidence of meaning. The study of music and sound, and the connection with craft activity should provide valuable evidence of meaning of another kind, this time, aural.

I have aimed at providing as detailed a description as possible of tested instruments which can succeed musically if the diagrams and instructions are followed.

Small diagrams within the text give details of some of the items, not necessarily the simplest. When it is necessary to have measured drawings they are provided on a large sheet in the pocket at the end of the book. Most of these measured drawings are full size and templates may be made from them very easily and accurately. I have made no attempt to separate the work for various age levels because teachers will easily decide whether or not work is suitable for their classes. Equipment and facilities are often the deciding factors. Chapters one to three give the instructions for making instruments. Chapter four discusses the materials available for instrument-making, and chapter five describes classroom and work-shop activities which demonstrate the production of sound from simple materials. Many of the suggestions made in these chapters may be carried much further and linked with science and mathematics.

These instruments are not intended to replace voice, pipe, recorder or existing percussion, but may be used in conjunction with all these means of musical expression, adding more colour and texture. Above all, I hope to provide teachers of music with material which may influence children's attitude to music for life by giving enjoyable instrumental experiences at an early age. Teaching music, and this includes the teaching of notation, through musical performance, is possible when the instruments provided are simple enough to be played soon after their introduction.

It is essential for the children to become aware of the full musical intent so that craft interest and romantic appeal are not alone in providing the impulse to build and possess musical instruments.

Note on the Author

A craftsman with an interest in music, Mr. Roberts has built violins, violas, spinets and harps. As a luthier, he has a particular enthusiasm for the viola. He has lectured, conducted teachers' courses and taken part in radio and television programmes in this country and abroad.

All the drawings, diagrams and photographs throughout the book, with the exception of plate 1 (frontispiece), are the work of the author.

CHAPTER ONE

Unpitched percussion instruments

THIS chapter presents unpitched percussion material ranging from items easily collected by the children themselves to articles which may be made only by secondary boys who have access to a school workshop.

Provision of rhythmic material for infant and early primary classes should be made on the basis that every member of a group should have the means of adding to the sound effect. Many of the items need to be made in sets of eight or ten to form sections of the ensemble. No attempt is made to separate infant from primary material because much of it covers both age ranges. It is possible to make some items with the simple tools that a primary class often has available today. Children will readily collect and assemble groups of the items needed, and will often be able to do much of the work of the more difficult items if the teacher in charge will complete the work. Taking part in such work satisfies almost as much as completing the construction, if the article is seen to grow within the classroom.

Shells

These may be collected in similar-sized pairs and used to tap one against another.

Pebbles

Collected and used in the same way.

Castanet type blocks

Each block has a hollow face. Build the blocks on bases of hardwood $2'' \times 2'' \times \frac{3}{8}''$ and add rims from hardwood $\frac{3}{8}'' \times \frac{3}{8}''$ in section. Glue short lengths of the square-section wood to the bases as shown in diagram 1. Use Cascamite or Unibond and allow the glue to set before grinding the meeting faces flat on a sheet of no. 1 glasspaper. This work may well be done in the primary class because it involves only simple sawing and glueing.

Diagram 2 shows a block of hardwood $2'' \times 2'' \times \frac{3}{4}''$ with a hollow bored on one side with a $1\frac{1}{2}''$ centre bit or gouged out with a $\frac{1}{2}''$ firmer gouge. Work of this kind

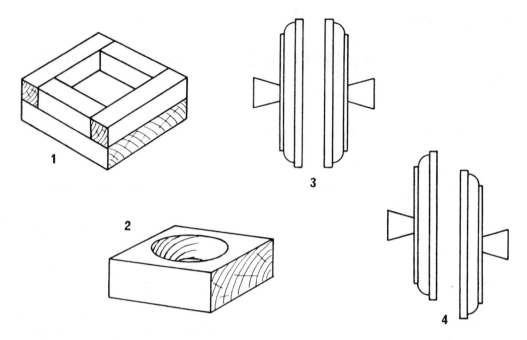

needs a vice and may be outside the range of primary work.

The kind of block used by electricians to mount ceiling roses or switches may also be bought and made into efficient rhythm blocks. These blocks have hollow undersides and may be fitted quite easily with small screw-in knobs which may be bought on the hardware counter. A pair of these makes a satisfying clapping sound and the tone may be varied by using direct contact as in diagram 3 or by clapping them with a small amount of overlap as in diagram 4.

Coconut shells

Pairs of half shells will provide deeper pitch and greater volume of sound and one or two pairs will be enough for one group. Variations in sound may be achieved with these items too.

Claves or rhythm sticks

Pairs of sticks cut from $\frac{5}{8}''$, $\frac{3}{4}''$ and $1''$ diameter hardwood dowel are useful items. Dowel rod may be bought from most craft shops and it should be cut into $7''$ or $8''$ lengths with a miniature hacksaw or with a small tenon saw. Use a bench-hook or sawing block whilst you saw. Inexperienced sawyers usually expend more energy in holding the wood than in sawing it. The bench-hook steadies the whole operation with far less effort. Smooth the cut ends with no. 1 glasspaper so that splinters give no trouble. Better claves may be made from a hard and resonant wood such as Honduras or Brazilian rosewood. This should be planed (or turned if a lathe is available) in short lengths, to diameters $\frac{5}{8}''$ to $1''$ and used in the same way as the common dowels. Some experiment with various lengths is suggested.

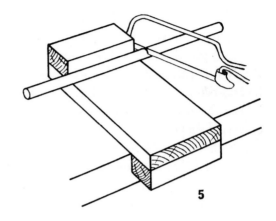

5

In playing, support one stick loosely between the finger tips and the fleshy base of the thumb of the left hand. Strike loosely with the other stick. The hollow of the partly closed left hand acts as a resonant chamber and gives amplification.

Shakers

These are easy to produce, even in the lower primary classes. The containers may vary in material and size and the contents too may vary. Many different effects may be produced. Containers may be:

Tins, the lids sealed with self-adhesive tape.

Plastic bottles or jars with screw tops. Some of these may be of the soft plastic type, others of the thinner and harder plastic. The screw-on caps should be glued in place and handles may be fitted to the caps to make rhythmic movement easy.

Maracas

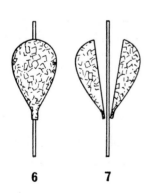

6 7

'Gourds' made from paper strips provide a substitute for the natural gourds which cannot easily be obtained in this country. Model a double-fist-size piece of Plasticine or clay to the shape and glue layers of paper over the form in the same way that glove puppet heads are often made. Use Cascamite glue and soak each short piece of paper in the glue so that the final thickness of paper will be well impregnated. The hardness of the glue will give good resonance. After about four layers of paper have been glued on and the glue is set, cut the shell longitudinally and remove the Plasticine before re-assembling the two halves to enclose a length of dowel about 18″ long. More strips of glued paper will strengthen the joint and glue the shell to the handle. Partly fill with lead shot before assembly and strengthen the whole with another layer or two of paper strips. Painting and decoration should complete this 'maraca'. See diagrams 6 and 7. The Plasticine may be used many times for maracas of varied shape.

Another type of hollow shell for a maraca may be made by glueing short lengths of 1″ bandage on an inflated rubber balloon. Cascamite should be used and the bandage strips should overlap one another. When the glue is set, the deflated balloon should be removed before the handle is glued in place.

Bamboo shakers

These are lengths of bamboo with natural node closures at one end and corks glued in the other. Bind the open end of the bamboo tightly with self-adhesive tape before putting in the loose contents and glueing in the cork; this will prevent a split in the cane. Bamboo of at least 1¼″ diameter is suitable. There must be room for the contents to move when the cane is shaken.

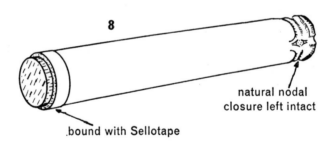

natural nodal
closure left intact

bound with Sellotape

FILLERS. Rice, grit, peas, small beans, small pieces of cork or hard felt (for tins only), lead shot (with adequate safeguard against mis-use by younger children). Containers need to be less than ⅛ full so that there is room for movement of the particles inside the containers. The fillers should not be mixed.

Jingles

Two effective jingles may be made in the classroom from simple materials. Both devices may have arms or other extensions added to make them into decorative central features of a group of players.

The Lagerphone or Jingling Johnnie

This consists of a broom handle covered from top to bottom with crown stoppers nailed loosely to the wood. It provides a rhythmical background. See plate 3.

Remove all traces of cork sealing and, with a stout nail, punch a hole centrally through each stopper. Nail the stoppers with ¾″ round-headed nails to the pole so that all are free to shake. Leave enough space for the broom handle to be held. Shoe the bottom of the pole with a rubber door stopper so that the hard 'thump' will be softened a little when the pole hits the floor.

The Milk rustle

This provides a rhythmic rustle and is even simpler to make. Collect about 200 *clean* aluminium caps from milk bottles and place them in a plastic bag of fair size—at least 18″ × 12″. Tie the open end. If room is left in the bag in which the caps can move, the whole may be shaken in various ways and provide an interesting background of sound for many activities.

Resonated jingles

In South America, jingles are made from nut shells strung together. Sometimes a resonator such as a gourd is surrounded by loose strings connecting the shells, berries, small bones or metal strips. The instrument is shaken rhythmically and the loose items tap against the hollow gourd.

A thinly turned beechwood bowl of 10″ or 12″ diameter may be fitted with a fell or vellum and small objects such as beans fastened loosely across this. This resonant shell would give sounds similar to those from a large gourd. Cheap drum vellums are available through the music shops. They should be soaked for about an hour before being stretched across the rim of the bowl. If many small holes are pricked along the edge of the skin, lacing of the skin to the bowl will be easy. See diagram 9. The tension should not be too great or the thin skin will tear as the drying shrinks it.

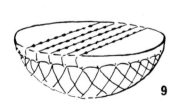

9

10

The container need not be round. A square or rectangular box about 10″ × 10″ × 3″ made from ½″ hardwood and with a bottom of 4 or 5 mm plywood would make the base for a resonated jingle. The head may be made from two thicknesses of tracing paper which sandwich a layer of mull or thin gauze. If the three layers are soaked well in Polycell they may be stretched across the open side of the box and the edges drawing-pinned down. The mull will then reinforce the paper. See diagram 10.

Simple drums

Single-headed drums may be made from tins, the smallest about 5″ long and 4″ in diameter. The open end may be fitted with three-layer heads as in the previous example. The edges of the 'sandwich' should be bound to the tin with a few turns of self-adhesive tape as the material dries. Paper alone may be used but then the head will not last long in class.

Larger double-headed drums may be made from tins and old *rubber* inner tubes from motor cars or even lorries. (Plastic tubes do not give a lively note.) Match the thickness of the rubber to the diameter of the tin. The biggest drum of this kind is made from a five-gallon floor-polish drum and a lorry inner tube.

Remove the top and bottom of the tin with a tin opener. The five-gallon drum will need a hammer and cold chisel for this operation. From the inner tube cut two discs, each 2″ greater in diameter than that of the tin. The discs may not lie flat but the tendency to curl should be ignored. Place the end of the tin concentrically on each disc in turn. Mark a pencil line about ¼″ outside the tin line and then step out on this line with dividers an *even* number of equidistant points, perhaps 18, 24 or 28 according to the size of the tin. The distance between points should be about 1″. With a pair of punch pliers cut ⅛″ holes in the rubber at these points and thread through them a thin, strong string which should be tied with a reef knot, but not until the discs are in place on the open ends of the tin. See diagram 11. A mason's line from the tool merchant will provide string of the right strength for this work but the lashing which follows will need a thicker cord. This should be more decorative and the colour may be chosen to fit the colour scheme of the finished drum. Before fitting the heads, band the outside of the tin with coloured paper or with a prepared decorative cover.

Several feet of medium blind cord will be needed for the zig-zag lashing which links the top and bottom lines of the thinner lacing. Tension this cord gradually, after lashing, and test the notes given by the rubber heads. There should be a lively response from light blows with a drum stick. If enough holes have been made in

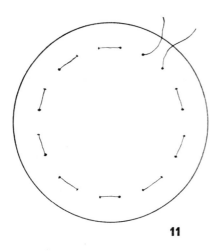

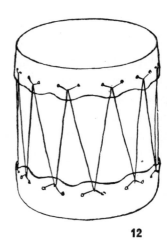

11   12

the discs, the thinner string will not tear the rubber. The tension of the lashing should be increased if the note is at all woolly. Tie the ends of the lashing into a bow or tassel or make provision with them for a shoulder loop.

Drum sticks

Sticks may be made from 10″ lengths of ⅜″ dowel with rounded ends. Larger drums will need 10″ lengths of 3/16″ diameter cane and 1″ wooden balls bored to take the cane and a little glue.

Drums with real vellums

The simple drums already described may be made in the primary school or where there is no provision for more difficult practical work. In the secondary school with workshops it is possible to build larger drums that have thicker natural skins than those mentioned in the description of the resonated jingle. Cylinders may be bent from 4 mm plywood and the ends joined by a glued scarf joint. See diagram 14 for the method of glueing and cramping the scarf joint. The cramping boards are shaped to fit the arc of the cylinder and paper is used to prevent the cramping boards from adhering to the plywood when the excess glue oozes out.

Larger drum vellums may be bought from the music shops, the cheaper ones from Pakistan and India. These may not be so even in thickness as the more expensive, professional quality skins but they give good service. Plastic 'vellums' are also on sale and these are ready lapped to metal hoops and may be fitted easily to prepared *shells*. This is the usual name for drum bodies.

If wood hoops and rims are needed, serviceable ones may be made by steaming and bending straight-grained beechwood. The meeting ends should be scarfed and glued together with one of the modern glues. Even willow withies may be soaked, bent and whipped with stout thread into hoops to which suitable vellums may be lapped.

Dimensions of drums of useful sizes are given in a table in this section. The largest one may also be made with double fell and deeper shell. It should give a good bass note. The range of single-headed drums is useful because it is possible to have some control over the pitch of each drum. Of course, no drum of this kind can compare with the real timpani because such kettle drums have domed shells which reflect in exactly the right way.

It has been found difficult to buy the screw adjusters needed for full control over the tension of the heads on this type of drum but it will be found that zig-zag lashing with sliding toggles gives quite a good variation in tension. Some suggestions are given for those who may wish to make the screw fittings in the school workshop. If mild steel is used for this work it is necessary to finish it free from sharp edges that may scratch the players or tear clothing. Some kind of lacquer is essential unless electro-plating can be arranged.

Young people should be encouraged to reduce the tension on drums when playing is finished. The instruments must be kept away from radiators and stoves, and should not be stored in damp places. This kind of care is valuable when professional, and therefore costly, timpani are encountered later. Early training can

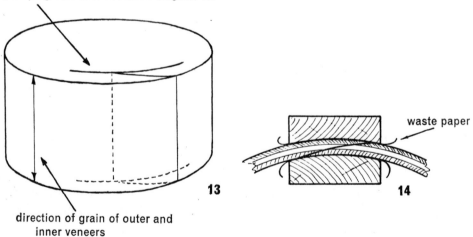

Thickness of plywood is exaggerated to show scarf. A section of this joint between cramping blocks is shown in diagram 14.

13

waste paper

14

direction of grain of outer and inner veneers

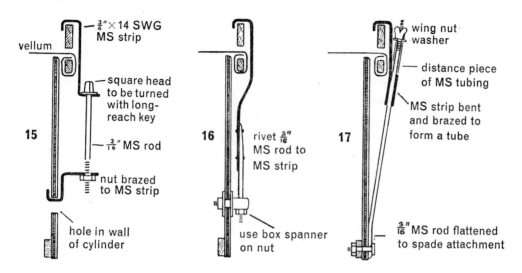

prevent expensive and inconvenient repairs.

The making of the middle drum of the three single-headed drums is described but the same methods apply to the other two. To save further drawings, the basic sizes of the four are given in table form. The last is the double-fell drum.

	No. of screws	Diam.	Ht.	Plywood	Beech for hoops	Beech for reinforcing hoops	Vellum size
1	5	$9\frac{7}{8}''$	$6\frac{3}{4}''$	$6\frac{3}{4}'' \times 32'' \times 3$ mm	$40'' \times 1\frac{3}{4}'' \times \frac{3}{16}''$	$40'' \times \frac{3}{4}'' \times \frac{3}{16}''$	$14''$
2	7	$13\frac{3}{4}''$	$8''$	$8'' \times 48'' \times 4$ mm	$56'' \times 2'' \times \frac{1}{4}''$	$56'' \times 1'' \times \frac{1}{4}''$	$18''$
3	9	$19\frac{3}{4}''$	$11\frac{1}{4}''$	$68'' \times 11\frac{1}{4}'' \times 4$ mm	$76'' \times 2\frac{1}{4}'' \times \frac{1}{4}''$	$72'' \times 1\frac{1}{4}'' \times \frac{1}{4}''$	$24''$
4	9	$19\frac{3}{4}''$	$15''$	$68'' \times 15'' \times 4$ mm	$76'' \times 2\frac{1}{4}'' \times \frac{1}{4}''$ (2)	$72'' \times 1\frac{1}{4}'' \times \frac{1}{4}''$ (2)	$24''$ (2)

CONSTRUCTION OF DRUM NO. 2 in the table of sizes and materials.

Cut a piece of plywood 8″ long × 48″ wide × 4 mm thickness. The size is expressed in this way so that the middle veneer of the three will run around the shell. The other two will then run vertically. It will be easier to bend the plywood if this arrangement is made. Not every piece of 4 mm plywood is suitable for such a tight bend as a 14″ diameter needs. Some warming and damping may be necessary. Trial bending should be done with the offcuts, if possible. Birch plywood barely 4 mm thick has been used successfully but it may be necessary to test several kinds of plywood. The small drum may need 3 mm plywood. It is a good plan to have spare material when making drums because some bends may fracture. Scarf and glue the joint (diagrams 13 and 14) and in cleaning, after the glue has set, remove the outer sharp edge so that it cannot cut the vellum.

Straight-grained kiln-dried Slavonian beech $56'' \times 1\frac{1}{2}'' \times \frac{1}{4}''$ will make a lapping hoop $\frac{3}{8}''$ wide and a matching pressure hoop about $\frac{7}{8}''$ wide. A 56'' piece seems to be longer than is necessary but the spare length is added so that in the hurried bending after steaming, the ends may be taken past one another to form a continuous curve. See diagram 18. Place on the drum a few layers of newspaper and fit the hoop to this oversize state. This will ensure that the finished hoops will fit over the bared drum and give clearance for some thickness of vellum. Scarf a joint and glue it after the steam moisture has dried out for a whole day. The scarf should be a close, well-fitting joint between 4'' and 5'' long. When the glue is set, part the narrow hoop longitudinally from the whole width with a sharp tenon saw.

The inner reinforcing rim need be only 1'' wide but coincidence between the joints on drum and rim should be avoided. Pin and glue the rim inside the drum; the prepared rim joint may be glued as the rim and drum are glued together. This will ensure a close fit along the circumference. Diagrams 15 to 17 show this type of rim in place.

An 18'' diameter vellum will be needed, allowing the usual 4'' in excess of drum diameter. Lapping a head is not so difficult as it may seem. Avoid sharp lapping tools and sharp edges on the hoop. The smooth handle ends of spoons are useful as tools and old toothbrush handles filed to thinner section and bent a little at the ends enable one to reach round the hoop and push the skin ends into place. Hot water will usually soften a handle for bending. Look also at diagrams 15 to 17. These show the placing of the lapped ends in their finished state.

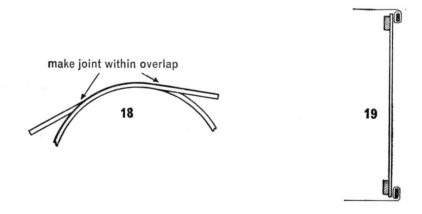

make joint within overlap

18

19

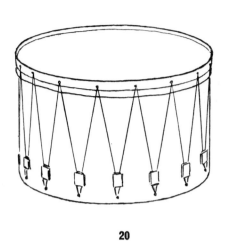

20   21

A well-shaped hoop in the first place helps to keep a good circle and this helps the even tensioning of the head when all is assembled. Work on a zinc or lino table top so that the fell may be kept moist during the lapping. If one of the resin glues has been used on a good hoop scarf, there need be no fear that the joint will spring as a result of using water to keep the fell moist.

With drum no. 4, the reinforcing hoops should be pinned and glued about ¼" below and inside the edges of each face so that there is no possibility that the heads will rattle against these extra rims. See diagram 19.

Zig-zag lashing on a drum can be very attractive, especially if a colour scheme is prepared. The cords and toggles form a regular pattern which always seems far more attractive than screw attachments, however efficient these metal devices may be. Two arrangements are shown in diagrams 20 and 21, one for a single fell drum, the other for a double. Almost twice the number of attachment points is needed when cords, instead of screws, are used. Nearly all closed drums give a better note if a small hole is drilled somewhere in the shell wall.

Pitch fibre drums

In their book on making simple musical instruments, Mandell and Wood describe a series of narrow drums built on pitch fibre piping. This kind of piping is available in diameters of 4″ and 6″ from builders' merchants in this country. The outside diameters are about 4¾″ and 7¼″. The walls of the pipe are thick. Drums made from this material are heavy but good results are possible. Almost exact instructions are given in this American book for 'tacked' drums, as opposed to lashed drums which

14 SWG
MS

22

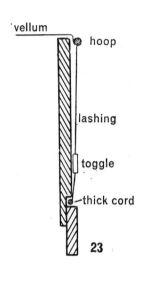

vellum

hoop

lashing

toggle

thick cord

23

use hoops. With a tacked drum, no adjustment of vellum tension is possible. If adjustment of vellum tension is essential, hoops and lashing must be provided and some provision must be made to anchor the lashing. Cords which passed through small holes in the pipe walls would slowly elongate the holes because of the semi-hard nature of the pitch fibre; metal flanges as the example shown in diagram 22 would engage the lower edge of the pipe and provide safer anchorages. Alternatively, by using the flange recess as shown in diagram 23, the lashings may be anchored safely to a band of thicker cord fitted in between the loose flange and the existing rebate on the pipe. The British pipes come with a loose flange at one end and this increased diameter may be used as a wider base on which the drum will stand more safely. The vellum itself may be lapped to a hoop steamed and bent to a circle, from beechwood of $\frac{1}{4}'' \times \frac{3}{16}''$ section. Alternatively, a willow withy may be used for the hoop. The withy should be soaked, bent, scarfed, glued and whipped so that its inside diameter is slightly larger than the outside diameter of the pipe.

Drum sticks

A variety of sticks is necessary. Those simple sticks made for the simple rubber-headed drums will be useful on occasion for the bigger drums, but usually a more weighty and woolly knop is needed. The sticks should be 12″ or 14″ long and of dowel or cane $\frac{5}{16}''$ or $\frac{3}{8}''$ in diameter. Medium or soft knops may be made by glueing a cork to the end of the stick and then wrapping and glueing felt strips around, finishing the outside to a diameter of about 1½″. Cover the whole knop with a cloth or stocking layer and whip the ends around the stick.

If more weight is needed, a rubber doorstop may be used instead of a cork. Enlarge the screw hole in the rubber with the tang of a file and glue the stick in the hole with Evostik.

Foam plastic or rubber may also be used to cover a central mass, and the whole then covered with fabric or knitted material.

Slit drums

Three kinds of slit drum may be made in the school workshop. The first kind needs a hardwood box construction, preferably with dovetailed corners and with top and bottom of 4 mm plywood. The joints should be snug and well glued and the top and bottom edges of the frame should be trued very carefully before the plywood is glued in place. (If a large sanding disc were available, this task would be made quick and easy). Avoid the use of pins and nails if possible; snug joints well glued with stout Cascamite are much better. See diagram 24.

A smaller, higher-pitched slit drum may be made from a block of hard, resonant wood such as Honduras or Brazilian rosewood, boxwood or walnut about $5'' \times 3'' \times 1\frac{3}{8}''$. Two $\frac{1}{4}''$ stopped mortises are chopped cleanly into the block, as the section shows in diagram 26. The mortises should not meet. Alternatively, the block may be 'fabricated' or built up from thinner pieces of wood and glued into one block. This fabrication would solve the problem of cutting deep, clean mortises. The finished block is shown in diagram 25.

The third kind of slit drum may be made from a length of $1\frac{1}{4}''$ or $1\frac{1}{2}''$ diameter bamboo. Cut a length of bamboo that encloses a hollow between two natural nodes. See diagram 27. With a sharp tenon saw cut a longitudinal slot $\frac{3}{16}''$ wide after drilling the ends of the marked position. Two parallel cuts should remove the waste. Bamboo is extremely hard on the surface and it may be found difficult

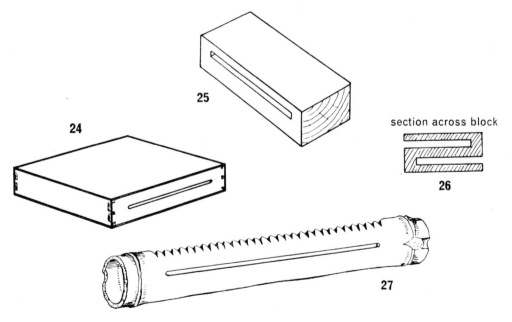

25

section across block

26

24

27

to start the saw on this natural enamel; the tip of the saw needs to be sharp. It is so easy to split bamboo in a woodwork vice and great care should be taken in gripping the material. A cracked length will give a cracked note. If several slit drums are being made, try some variation in the width of the slots. Lightweight sticks with hard knops will be needed to sound this type of percussion instrument.

Rasp or Guiro

The bamboo type of slit drum is easily made into a rasp. Diagram 27 shows a line of ridges cut along the same piece of bamboo. A rough square section file or the corner of a rough flat file is needed for this notching. A bench hook will help to hold the bamboo during this process. The characteristic sound of the instrument is produced by rubbing a stick along the notches. Part of the sound comes from the stick and trials should be made with sticks of varying thickness and stiffness.

CHAPTER TWO

Pitched percussion instruments

NEARLY all the instruments described so far have been without positive pitch. Only the single-headed drums, perhaps, give an actual note, and this only if the tension and thickness of the head are correct and the exact point of strike is found. The addition of actual notes to existing percussion work can be a vital step in making music. This addition satisfies children and gives opportunity for further musical development.

Plant pots

It is easy to start with a few unglazed plant pots chosen to sound two or three notes. One should provide a visual as well as an aural guide to the use of pots by choosing the pots carefully; a small pot should give a higher note than a large one. The association between size and pitch is important. It is not always the largest pot in a random group which gives the lowest note. The chosen pots may be hung on strings threaded through the drainage holes and tied to a stick.

To choose a full octave from the stock of pots in a seedsman's shop would take a long time, especially if the notes had to match the notes given by existing instruments. On the other hand, a random group of pots might provide an effect like that given by the 'slung mugs' in 'Noyes Fludde'. Notes which are wide of the mark would probably sound better than notes which are nearly correct. The 2″ and 2½″ diameter pots are better than the 'thumbs'. Small toggles of about pencil thickness should be tied to the strings inside the pots to suspend them like bells.

Glass tumblers

Glass containers of this kind may be partly filled with water and tuned to provide notes. These items must be set up each time they are needed but the plant pots may be left suspended or stored in a cupboard.

Simple xylophones of softwood

The tone of these instruments is not so round as that of the hardwood instruments. The notes given are more staccato, partly because of the absence of the resonance chambers. The instruments are easy to make if the timber is bought ready planed on all four faces to the section stated, but skill is needed in tuning. The pitch of these instruments in use should be checked occasionally because continued hammering with hard beaters may reduce the cross-section in the middle of each batten; the pitch may therefore fall a little over a period of a few weeks. Battens of the hardwood xylophone do not suffer in this way.

State exactly the finished section size, the name of the wood and the quality, e.g. straight-grained, free from knots and shakes (cracks). This quality is sometimes charged as 'selected', 'cleaner and better', or 'straight and clear'. Before ordering, find out what lengths are available in the timber chosen. The Columbian pine for the simple xylophone, for instance, is often available in 16' or 18' lengths but 10' lengths would be more convenient to use in school. The scarcer jacaranda for the resonated xylophone comes in short billets and one is lucky to get even 4' lengths.

The habit should be formed of marking and cutting off the longer pieces first and then scheming the shorter pieces from what is left; otherwise there will be waste. The charge on the account is often expressed *per foot run*: for example 7d or 8d *per foot run* of a section $\frac{7}{8}'' \times \frac{7}{8}''$. This means that every lineal foot of the delivered material is charged at 7d or 8d. One may never know the cross-section size of the board or plank from which the smaller-sectioned material has been sawn and planed. Some merchants may charge instead for the original plank of pine, perhaps an 8' length of $10'' \times 2''$ section and then charge extra for machine work in sawing and planing. 'Offcuts' from the 8' length, that is, pieces neither wide nor thick enough to fulfil the specification of the section ordered, are often delivered with the goods when this method of charging is used.

Find some well-seasoned Columbian pine (Douglas fir) for the simple xylophone and, before ordering a large quantity, order a few feet of $\frac{7}{8}'' \times \frac{7}{8}''$ section, exactly square. This is for trials of tone. If it is possible to select the actual board, choose one which is a uniform marmalade colour rather than a pink one or one showing both coloured wood and white bands of sapwood. If some of the longer battens give reasonable tone without two-note effects, order the rest of the wood needed. This would be prepared from a 1'' rough-sawn board. If there is any doubt about the seasoned state of the wood, order in good time and allow the stock to remain for several weeks in the same kind of warmth and atmosphere as the classrooms have. The drying out of moisture from a tuned batten can alter the pitch of the note given.

MAKING A SOFTWOOD XYLOPHONE a′ TO a‴. The stand and beaters must be made before the battens can be sounded. Make the stand from four lengths of $1″ \times \frac{1}{4}″$ red deal lath, free from knots. The lath need not be planed but sharp edges should be smoothed with glasspaper. Red deal is better than offcuts from the Columbian pine because it is less likely to split when the pinning is done. Cut two pieces 16″ long, one piece $8\frac{3}{4}″$, and one $4\frac{1}{2}″$, and glue and pin the frame together with a few $\frac{1}{2}″ \times 19$ SWG panel pins. Look at diagram 28. If the pin points come through, clench them between the hammer and an old flat-iron. Cover the wooden bearing surfaces with strips cut from a cheap foam plastic bath mat, glueing the strips to the frame with Evostik. For beaters, use two lengths of $\frac{3}{16}″$ diameter cane and two 1″ wooden balls from a craft shop.

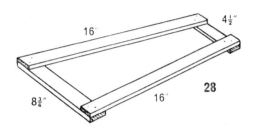

Drill holes in the balls and glue the ends of the cane in place. The xylophone is always played with at least two beaters.

The lengths shown in the table are *approximate*. Wood varies in density and texture and because of this variation, pieces of the same length and cross-section cut from the same tree may give quite different notes. Each piece of wood used may need to be *longer* or *shorter* than the lengths given.

	Helmholtz notation	*Approximate* lengths of $\frac{7}{8}″ \times \frac{7}{8}″$ Columbian pine to give these notes (total length about 14′).
High soh	a‴	$6\frac{3}{4}″$
	g‴	$7\frac{1}{8}″$
	f‴♯	$7\frac{3}{8}″$
	e‴	$7\frac{3}{4}″$
doh′	d‴	$8\frac{3}{8}″$
	c‴♯	$8\frac{1}{2}″$
	b″	$9\frac{1}{4}″$
One-octave diatonic	a″	$9\frac{5}{8}″$
	g″	$10\frac{1}{4}″$
	f″♯	$10\frac{3}{4}″$
	e″	$11\frac{1}{2}″$
doh	d″	$12\frac{1}{8}″$
	c″♯	$12\frac{7}{8}″$
	b′	$13\frac{1}{2}″$
Low soh	a′	$14\frac{1}{4}″$ Begin with this piece.

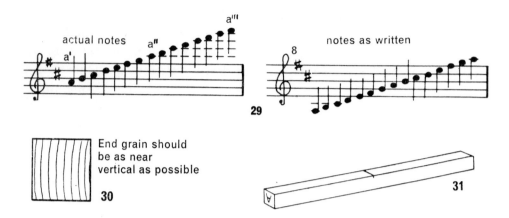

actual notes

notes as written

29

End grain should
be as near
vertical as possible

30

31

Some pieces of wood may give false or double notes and these pieces must be discarded. Arrange the cross-section of the battens so that the narrow edges of the growth rings face the top. See diagram 30. Mark the end grain of each piece so that this position may be recognised. A batten placed on one of the other faces may give quite a different note; this can be confusing when a scale is being laid.

Using a bench hook and a sharp tenon saw or an Eclipse miniature hacksaw, cut from the stock length the longest batten ½″ longer than the stated length. Cut cleanly and squarely, trying to avoid splintered ends. Lay the batten on the foam-covered stand, making sure that the narrow grain is uppermost. Mark the end with soft pencil. Strike the middle of the wood with a beater and listen to the note. It will probably be lower than the a′ needed. If it is low, shorten the batten by ¼″, strike and listen again. The pitch should have risen slightly. Continue to shorten and strike until you think the note is correct but take care to reduce length by very small amounts in the final stages. Perhaps only sixteenths of an inch need be cut off towards the end of the tuning. If the note has risen too far in pitch, it may be flattened by sawing across the *underside* of the batten a shallow cut. This is a very delicate task because the shallowest cut will lower the pitch considerably. This *kerf* virtually reduces the cross-section measurement at the midpoint. Study diagram 31.

Take the next batten, the b′, and tune this in the same way. Tune the remainder, in turn, making any length allowances that the nature of the timber seems to need. The upper notes seem to need even more careful tuning than the lower. When the scale is complete, play a few tunes on the xylophone; this will test the intervals.

The tuning of a xylophone calls for concentration and if too many people are trying to tune at the same time there will be some confusion. The sound from wood is soon dispersed: there is no prolongation. The batten to be tuned and the note which is known to be correct should be played almost at the same time; otherwise one must depend too much upon memory. Skill in recognising small differences of pitch should grow after a few notes have been tuned successfully.

An instrument with a scale of D major is described but it is not essential to use this key. It is here as an example but it may be found very useful as it stands. If C major or other keys are required, slight adjustments should be made to the table of lengths given.

At this stage it is well to consider the standard of pitch of your instruments. If you already possess tuned percussion instruments and you are tuning to match these, they will almost certainly be tuned to a' 440. This pitch is accepted today as an international standard. If you tune to a piano it is by no means certain that your piano is of this standard pitch. Much of the work with tuned percussion may be done without piano but it would be an advantage to have all the instruments of the same pitch. A problem of this kind might provide an incentive to have the piano brought to the modern a' 440. This would be a good step, provided that the piano would withstand the strain of the change. Standardisation brings the advantages of interchange of all instruments within the school and between schools.

If you have worked cleanly, the battens will need very little cleaning but sharp edges should be removed with fine glasspaper. Do not take off too much wood with the abrasive or the pitch will fall because of the reduced cross-section. Name each note neatly on the upper surface with a felt pen and polish all battens with a prepared wax polish. The polishing seems to brighten the tone and you will also hear the improvement in tone when you lay the battens on the stand in good order. The space enclosed under the wood seems to act as a resonant chamber or

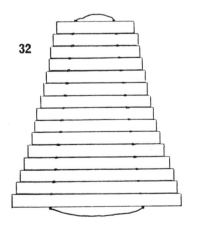

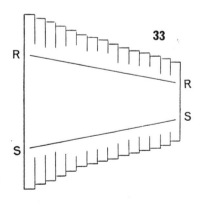

soundbox. You may prove this easily by playing with and without the stand.

It is a good thing to connect quite loosely the battens of these softwood xylophones. The instruments are more easily picked up and vital notes are not mislaid. The disadvantage is that the interchangeability of the battens disappears; all must be laid out each time the instrument is played and no change of key by changing battens is possible. These xylophones could be reserved for children who have passed the stage when numbers of separable notes are needed. Diagram 32 shows an assembled instrument.

To mark out the holes, turn each batten through 90° to the left so that the broad-grained sides are uppermost. Mark on each outer batten the two nodal points R and S 22% of the length from the ends. A distance slightly less than a quarter of the length may be judged. Join with soft pencil and straightedge each pair of outer points as shown: R to R and S to S. See diagram 33. Use *faint* pencil lines. Drill centrally through each batten a $\frac{5}{64}''$ hole to take a medium blind cord. A wheel brace and $\frac{5}{64}''$ carbon steel drill will do this better than a carpenter's brace and bit. If a pillar drill and power are available, time can be saved. If these holes are drilled in the correct positions, the pitch of the instrument will not be altered.

Felt washers will be needed to separate the battens on the cord and these can be cut from an old felt hat with a pair of scissors. If many washers are needed, it will save time to buy a $\frac{3}{8}''$ or $\frac{1}{2}''$ wad punch and use this on the *end grain* of a block of beech or oak. A cheap and effective wad punch may be made from a short length of steel conduit. File one end to a cutting edge. When the washer discs have been cut, the central hole in each should be cut with a pair of punch pliers.

Assemble the battens, washers and cord and leave a loop at each end to facilitate handling.

Smaller xylophones of softwood

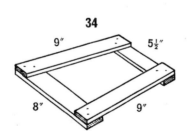

If you wish to make a smaller xylophone of this kind, choose the notes and make a foam-covered frame similar to the large one. Diagram 34 shows a stand suitable for a one-octave instrument c″ to c‴. Support for the battens must be as near as possible at the nodal points. (There are interesting differences between the nodes on a vibrating string and those on a rigid bar).

A two-note xylophone on a cord

A two-note suspended xylophone is easy to make. It may be held by the cord and struck with a single beater. No frame is needed. The timber used is again Columbian pine but it is planed this time to a section $1'' \times \frac{5}{8}''$, the narrow grain showing on the wider surfaces, if possible. The approximate lengths needed are $13\frac{3}{4}''$ for the d′ and $12\frac{1}{4}''$ for the g′. These wide and shallow pieces give deeper pitch than the square section material.

After being tuned to pitch by cutting off small amounts, the battens are looped into a pair by cord and small staples. Suspension points are at the nodes and the loop gives a safe grip for the left hand. The right hand holds the normal hard-headed beater. Diagrams 35 and 36 show both appearance and pitch. Note that Helmholtz notation is not used on the battens to indicate the notes.

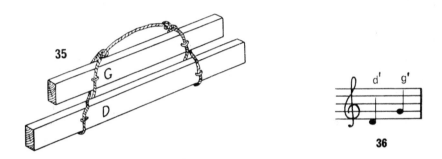

THE USE OF THE XYLOPHONES. Instruments of this kind may be used descriptively before they are used in concerted music. There are many opportunities during drama or the telling of stories. Examples are:

Water running over pebbles in a brook (light and rapid tapping with two beaters, up and down the battens)

Rowing in a boat (gentle swishing with beaters up and down)

Running and jumping—use of wide intervals

Walking upstairs—slowly, treading on each step or quickly, in bounds

The xylophones so far described can be made in the top class of a primary school, particularly by boys, if help is given in assembling and tuning.

A simple use for the two-note xylophone in ensemble is for stressing the pulse and harmonic accompaniment in a tune sung by a class. Such a song might be 'Bobby Shaftoe', in which the harmonic changes are regular and easily defined. In diagram 37 is given an example of this kind of use, only doh and low soh being used in the chorus. Monotony could be avoided by varying the rhythmic pattern

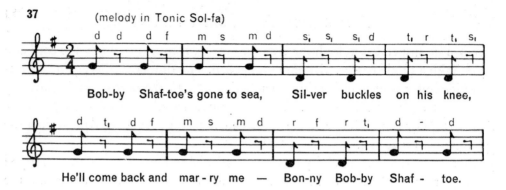

37 (melody in Tonic Sol-fa)

Bob-by Shaf-toe's gone to sea, Sil-ver buckles on his knee,

He'll come back and mar-ry me — Bon-ny Bob-by Shaf - toe.

of the accompaniment and by giving the class the verse to sing without accompaniment. The larger xylophone could be used in similar ways. When melodic use is undertaken, short phrases should be played at first.

A suitable second instrument to play with the voice and the xylophone is either the glockenspiel or the metallophone. The tone contrast brought by these metal instruments, together with the sustained notes that they give, enables a variety of treatment to be given to a song. Children enjoy suggesting arrangements for this work.

Resonated xylophone

Workshop facilities are needed for the making of this instrument. The battens are of hardwood and the box needs to be soundly made. This box has several floor levels so arranged that maximum resonance is given to groups of notes. Ideally, each batten should have its own compartment with a floor exactly at the right depth to emphasise and prolong the note given. The design given in the drawing is economic but quite efficient. Make the box from any well-seasoned softwood that is free from shakes. 'Live' knots, i.e. knots firmly fixed to the surrounding wood and not loose, will not spoil results. Corner joints may be (a) butted, glued and nailed or (b) dovetailed. Because the corners are nearly right-angles, one may safely ignore the few degrees of difference, whether the joints are dovetailed or nailed, if the end grain is well glued with Cascamite before assembly. The compartment dividers are housed and glued in place. The floors may be ledged, glued and pinned for quick assembly. There should be no trace of rattle when the box is finished.

There are two main timbers for the battens of the best resonated xylophones but three or four names are used to describe them. The most easily recognised is the Honduras or Brazilian rosewood and this is very hard and a pink-brown in colour. In some places I have seen this described as jacaranda. The other timber is

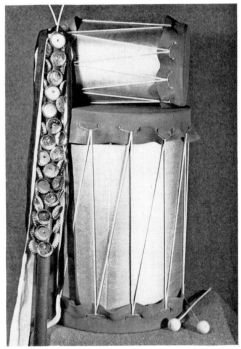

Plate 2. Completing the lashing on a simple drum. A 7lb. glue tin and a *rubber* inner tube from a motor car provide the main components.

Plate 3. The 'lagerphone' with simple drums. The large drum is made from a five-gallon tin and a *rubber* inner tube from a heavy vehicle.

Plate 4. Pre-boring the hitch pin holes on the simple psaltery. Note the slight tilt of the wheel-brace. The wrest pins have already been inserted at the far end of the psaltery.

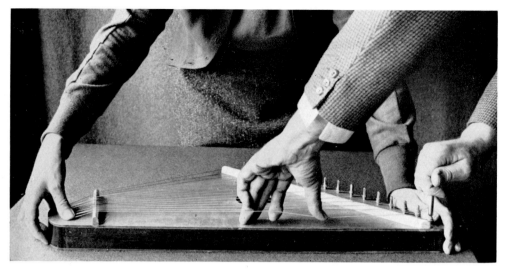

Plate 5. Mounting the last string on the lyre. The helper holds the box and with the right thumb ensures that the loop of the string remains on the hitch pin. The maker's left hand controls the string and allows the slack to be taken up by the wrest pin. This is the surest method of achieving neat coils on the wrest pin.

Plate 6. Bowing the lower C on the bowed psaltery. The psaltery shown is slightly longer than that described in the book. It has an extra string at the far end.

Plate 7. Knocking on a piece of softwood to hear the response. The wood is held loosely between thumb and middle finger.

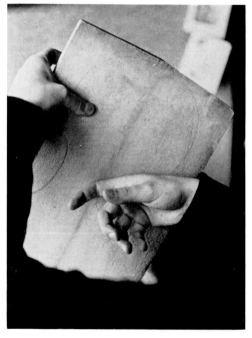

brown, with no trace of red and it has streaks and lines of charcoal grey and black, or bands of fairly light and very dark brown. It is not so hard as the first timber described and the last delivery was described as 'jacaranda'. This same timber is sometimes known as 'palissander'. Bombay rosewood is not as suitable for xylophone battens as the other two varieties mentioned.

The more usual timbers may be used if these special ones are not available or if the cost of them is too high. For instance, iroko and hard mahogany have been used successfully. Of the home-grown timbers, walnut is probably the best but this may be as scarce as the exotic imported timbers. Beech, plane, cherry, pear and a dense type of ash have all been used for battens. The near-oval section shown in the drawing on the large inserted sheet helps the tonal results, but this shape is not absolutely necessary if there are no opportunities to have the battens spindled to this section in a wood-machinists' shop. Some professional-standard xylophones have rectangular-sectioned battens with rounded or 'radiused' arrises.

Before cutting any battens, make the box and cover the top edges with foam plastic. At this stage, do not screw on the lifting ledges or fit the locating pins. Take all measurements for the box from the drawing on the inserted sheet at the end of the book.

MAKING THE BEATERS. Now make the special pair of strikers needed for the instrument. Hard felt seems to be the best material for the knops but it is difficult to obtain and in any case it is dear. It is not difficult to 'fabricate' knops from old felt hats or from leather. Discs may be cut with scissors and then glued together with Unibond or Evostik. See diagram 38. Final shaping should be done with coarse glasspaper when the glue is set. The knops should be about the size of pigeons' eggs. A central hole in each disc of felt or leather should take the end of a 12" length of $\frac{3}{16}$" cane or dowel.

Figure 39 shows a knop which is made from an isosceles triangle of felt or leather, the equal sides 8" or 10" long and the base 1". This triangle should be glued and rolled around the stick.

Rubber and cork have been used successfully for knops. Buy four 'Holdtite' $\frac{3}{4}$" tap washers from the hardware counter and with Evostik glue them together in pairs on the ends of the 12" sticks. Corks of 1" diameter may be domed with file and glasspaper and glued to sticks in the same way.

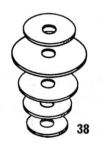 

BATTENS OR KEYS. The word 'battens' is used in preference to 'keys' so that there is no confusion with double meanings. Scheme the lengths from the stock material (longest pieces first) and saw them in one operation. There is no need to allow an extra length or to cut and tune alternately as with the softwood xylophone because the tuning is done entirely by cutting the underside and not by shortening the batten. Duplicate lengths should be cut for c′♯, f′♯, b′♭, c″♯ and f″♯ to provide accidentals. Avoid any obvious sapwood and shakes. When the battens are cut, remove sharp edges with no. 1 glasspaper and clean carefully with the same grade followed by finer paper. Choose the upper side of each for its grain and good appearance and pay particular attention to this surface. Try to remove the ripples left from the spindling if the stock has been machine-prepared; these will show up after polishing if they are not removed. The undersides will need little attention but they should not be left rough. A smooth finish helps the production of tone.

Table of batten lengths for the resonated xylophone:

Battens of prepared section (total length about 14′, allowing for some waste)
(See sheet of drawings for section)

a″	$6\frac{11}{16}″$
g″	$7″$
f″	$7\frac{5}{16}″$ Cut another for f″♯
e″	$7\frac{5}{8}″$
d″	$7\frac{15}{16}″$
c″	$8\frac{5}{16}″$ Cut another for c″♯
b′	$8\frac{11}{16}″$ Cut another for b′♭
a′ (440 c.p.s.)	$9″$
g′	$9\frac{3}{8}″$
f′	$9\frac{11}{16}″$ Cut another for f′♯
e′	$10″$
d′	$10\frac{5}{16}″$
c′ (middle C)	$10\frac{5}{8}″$ Cut another for c′♯

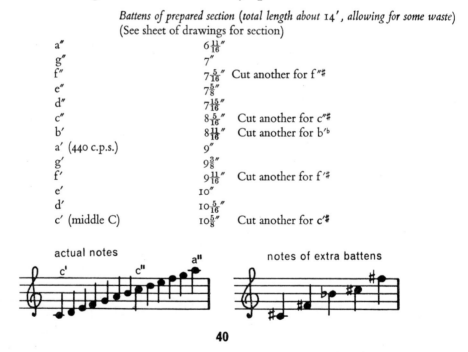

40

Lay the longest batten in its place on the box and strike it in the middle with a beater. The note given may be as much as five or six notes *higher* than the pitch required, middle C (c′ by Helmholtz). By reducing the thickness of the batten over the middle third of the length, this note may be brought down to the pitch required.

A Surform file will take off most of the waste if the batten is held firmly in a wood-faced vice. Tuning checks should be made frequently as the filing is done, to see that the pitch does not fall too low. A carbide cintride file followed by cabinet scraper and glasspaper should be used for the final tuning and finish. No guide can be given about the amount of wood to be taken off because the wood varies in texture and weight. Whatever the amount, the arc cut away should extend gracefully over the middle third of the length and should not be confined to a small portion of the batten. See diagrams 41 and 42.

The battens should be tuned in turn and checked carefully against a similar instrument or against a piano of standard pitch. Some people find it difficult to compare notes from instruments which have two completely different timbres, as with xylophone and pianoforte. They may find it easier to compare similar timbres, e.g. xylophone with xylophone. When all the battens have been tuned, fragments of tunes should be played in the keys of C, F, D and G to check the intervals. It is sometimes found that the basic key of C sounds well but when some of the same battens are used in a different key, the intervals do not please.

This instrument is very suitable for providing an ostinato accompaniment. The box may be stripped of all battens except for two, for instance, to provide a drone accompaniment of c' and g' or d' and a'. When only two notes are used, the only practical problem is that of timing. The playing of these notes in ensemble calls for little more technical skill than the playing of unpitched percussion instruments. The only difference is that each hand holds a striker.

The separable battens also allow a teacher to demonstrate visually and aurally the build-up of a scale. When the use of two notes has been explored, other notes may be added until a limited scale has been built up. Both pentatonic and diatonic scales may be used in this method of helping children towards musical understanding.

Note that the holes through the battens are at one end only. At the other end the battens lie unfixed between nails with rubber sleeves. Each batten is therefore easy to lift out and this feature makes the instrument readily adaptable for early exercises. Another advantage is that quick changes may be made into several other keys from the basic C major to which the instrument is tuned. It is easy, for instance, to lift out the b′ and replace it with b′ᵇ if the F major diatonic scale is needed.

The battens rest on strips of foam plastic glued with Evostik to the top edges of the box. The alternative to foam is two lengths of bicycle valve rubber tubing which run from end to end and pass around alternate location pins. Valve rubber is used also for the sleeves on the location pins. Each batten should be free to move slightly and should not be held at all rigidly by pins and sleeves. The hole in each batten may be drilled without altering the pitch if the right point is found: again, the nodal point.

Tubular glockenspiel

Small-bore aluminium alloy tubing gives good notes when it is cut to short lengths. Two sizes of tube are suitable, one with an inside diameter of $\frac{1}{2}$″ and the other with outside diameter $\frac{1}{2}$″. The tables give approximate lengths of tubing so that pieces may be cut and then adjusted to the notes required. Very slight variations in the manufacturer's finished cross-section give slight variations in pitch for a given length. In making this instrument no holes need to be drilled and this is an advantage when facilities are limited.

Make a stand first. This is a simple frame like the softwood xylophone stand and it supports at the nodal points of the tubes. Two sizes are given in diagrams 43 and 44. The construction is the same as in diagram 34.

Positioning of the tubes on the padded stand can be effected by glueing small pads of foam plastic on top of the long pads in such positions that adjacent tubes are separated. See diagram 45. These separators will not damp the notes too much.

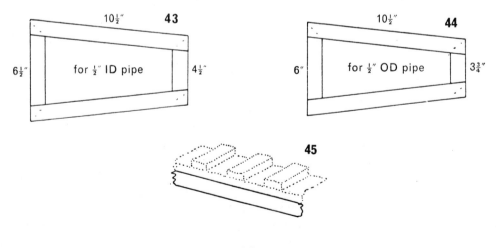

BEATERS. There should be two pairs of beaters to each instrument, one with wooden knops, the other with rubber. The instructions for making the hard beaters for the softwood xylophone are valid here; the rubber beaters are described in the section about the resonated xylophone.

TUBING NEEDED. The stock comes in 10′ lengths and any electrician should be able to supply it if an order is placed in good time.

CUTTING THE LENGTHS OF TUBING. The stock is easy to cut with an 'Eclipse' miniature hacksaw. Use, in addition, a bench-hook as recommended for holding dowel and xylophone stock. Start with the longest piece, the lowest note. A piece of tubing, $\frac{1}{16}$″ longer than the length stated, should be cut. The note this gives will probably be slightly flat in pitch when compared with the note stated in the table. The ends of the tube should be filed squarely to sharpen this note to reach the exact pitch. This filing will also remove sharp edges. A 6″ second-cut flat file will remove a little metal easily from the ends of the tube. Try to avoid the use of a vice in filing the ends of the tubing because the alloy is so soft that the tube is easily crushed. Take care over the tuning and ensure that the pitch matches existing instruments, whether tuned percussion or piano. If a note is sharpened by filing off too much metal, it should be used for the next tone or semitone higher in the scale. Diagram 46 on page 36 shows the full notation.

Even easier to use than a hacksaw is an 'Enox' no. 1 thin pipe cutter. This has two small rollers to hold the tube and a cutting disc which is advanced a small fraction of an inch at a time by means of a knurled nut. The rotary action of this tool cuts squarely and cleanly and only a small burr need be removed from the inner edge of the tube after a cut has been made. This rotary pipe cutter will not remove small pieces from the ends of the tubing.

Aluminium alloy tube, $\frac{1}{2}$″ inside diameter, 16 SWG walls			Aluminium alloy tube, $\frac{1}{2}$″ outside diameter, to BS 31/1940		
e''''	$7\frac{3}{16}$″		e''''	$6\frac{1}{16}$″	
d''''	$7\frac{5}{8}$″		d''''	$6\frac{5}{8}$″	
c''''	$8\frac{1}{8}$″	c''''♯ $7\frac{7}{8}$″	c''''	$7\frac{3}{16}$″	c''''♯ $6\frac{15}{16}$″
b'''	$8\frac{7}{16}$″	b'''♭ $8\frac{11}{16}$″	b'''	$7\frac{1}{2}$″	b'''♭ $7\frac{3}{4}$″
a'''	$8\frac{7}{8}$″		a'''	$7\frac{15}{16}$″	
g'''	$9\frac{7}{16}$″		g'''	$8\frac{9}{16}$″	
f'''	$9\frac{7}{8}$″	f'''♯ $9\frac{11}{16}$″	f'''	9″	f'''♯ $8\frac{3}{4}$″
e'''	$10\frac{1}{4}$″		e'''	$9\frac{3}{16}$″	
d'''	$10\frac{15}{16}$″		d'''	$9\frac{13}{16}$″	
c'''	$11\frac{5}{8}$″	c'''♯ $11\frac{3}{8}$″	c'''	$10\frac{3}{8}$″	c'''♯ $10\frac{1}{8}$″

The notes of the tubular glockenspiel sound *two octaves* higher than they are written.

46

The notes of the large metallophone sound *one octave* higher, the notes of the small metallophone sound *two octaves* higher than they are written.

47

Bar glockenspiel or metallophone

This instrument is cheaper to make than the tubular glockenspiel but it needs a more elaborate stand and more workmanship. Two sizes of instrument are described, one from c‴ to g⁗ in pitch and the other from c″ to g‴. The metal used is $\frac{3}{4}'' \times \frac{1}{8}''$ and $1'' \times \frac{1}{8}''$ 'commercial half-hard' aluminium bar. Less than half a pound is needed for the smaller instrument and about one pound for the other. The stock may be bought from the ironmonger in 12′ lengths. 'Soft' quality should not be accepted. A 12′ length of the narrow metal weighs about 18 oz; the wider weighs about $1\frac{1}{2}$ lb a length.

MATERIALS REQUIRED for glockenspiel stands

c‴ to g⁗	c″ to g‴
Base: 1 piece plywood $13'' \times 4'' \times \frac{3}{8}''$	1 piece $18'' \times 6'' \times \frac{3}{8}''$
Box sides: 2 pieces deal $12\frac{3}{8}'' \times 1'' \times \frac{1}{2}''$	2 pieces $17\frac{3}{16}'' \times 2'' \times \frac{1}{2}''$
Box end: 1 piece deal $2\frac{13}{16}'' \times 1'' \times \frac{1}{2}''$	1 piece $3\frac{5}{8}'' \times 2'' \times \frac{1}{2}''$
Box end: 1 piece deal $1'' \times 1'' \times \frac{1}{2}''$	1 piece $1\frac{5}{8}'' \times 2'' \times \ ''$
Top of 4 mm plywood to fit trapezoid	ditto
19 panel pins 1″ no. 16 SWG for location	ditto
1 dozen panel pins 1″ no. 18 SWG for joints	ditto
2 dozen panel pins $\frac{1}{2}''$ no. 19 SWG to fix top	ditto
6 countersink wood screws $\frac{3}{4}''$ no. 6 gauge	ditto
Foam plastic for strips under metal	ditto
Glue for the wood and Evostik for the foam	ditto

MAKING THE BOX OR STAND. This should be made first so that full resonance may be heard from the lengths of metal during the tuning process. Each length will have a quiet note until the resonance of the box amplifies it. Nail and glue the trapezoid frame together and mount it on the baseboard with nails or screws. Cut the plywood top to size and bore holes of the size shown so that each hole will be exactly under the mid-point of its appropriate metal bar. Pin and glue the top in place and use foam plastic to pad the edges of the box so that each length of metal will rest on its nodal points on a padding of foam. At this stage the locating pins should not be inserted. Read the appropriate drawing on the inserted sheet.

BEATERS. The instructions for the tubular glockenspiel beaters apply.

CUTTING THE LENGTHS. The lengths given in the tables are approximate. One may be lucky with a batch of aluminium and find that all the lengths given result in almost exactly the tuning required. The material seems to vary slightly in thickness towards the ends of the 12′ lengths in which it is supplied. Cut the c″ or the c‴ first, according to the size of the instrument chosen. Cut slightly longer than the size shown and file the ends to smooth them and to sharpen the note to the correct pitch. Use a bench shear or a miniature hacksaw to cut across the metal and a 6″ second-cut flat file to smooth the ends. If no vice is available, the usual bench-hook will help to hold the material. Rest each length on the padded box during the tuning process.

'Commercial half-hard' aluminium bar							
$\frac{3}{4}″ \times \frac{1}{8}″$				$1″ \times \frac{1}{8}″$			
g⁗	2 $\frac{27}{32}$″						
f‴	3 $\frac{1}{32}$″	f‴♯	2 $\frac{15}{16}$″				
e⁗	3 $\frac{3}{32}$″						
d⁗	3 $\frac{5}{16}$″						
c⁗	3 $\frac{15}{32}$″	c⁗♯	3 $\frac{3}{8}$″		A length of 8′ will make		
b‴	3 $\frac{9}{16}$″	b‴♭	3 $\frac{11}{16}$″		this instrument.		
a‴	3 $\frac{25}{32}$″						
g‴	4″			g‴	4 $\frac{1}{4}$″		
f‴	4 $\frac{1}{4}$″	f‴♯	4 $\frac{1}{8}$″	f‴	4 $\frac{7}{16}$″	f‴♯	4 $\frac{5}{16}$″
e‴	4 $\frac{7}{16}$″			e‴	4 $\frac{9}{16}$″		
d‴	4 $\frac{21}{32}$″			d‴	4 $\frac{15}{16}$″		
c‴	4 $\frac{15}{16}$″	c‴♯	4 $\frac{13}{16}$″	c‴	5 $\frac{1}{8}$″	c‴♯	5″
	A length of 6′ will make			b″	5 $\frac{1}{4}$″	b″♭	5 $\frac{3}{8}$″
	this instrument.			a″	5 $\frac{9}{16}$″		
				g″	6″		
				f″	6 $\frac{1}{4}$″	f″♯	6 $\frac{3}{16}$″
				e″	6 $\frac{5}{8}$″		
				d″	6 $\frac{7}{8}$″		
				c″	7 $\frac{1}{4}$″	c″♯	7″

Another advantage over the tubular instrument is that a length may be re-tuned after taking off too much metal and making the note too sharp. A notch may be filed at the midpoint on the *underside* of the metal to flatten the note in the same kind of correction that is recommended for the softwood xylophone. Only small corrections may be made in this way, perhaps less than quarter tones. See diagram 48.

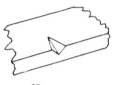

48

If several instruments of this kind are to be made, a master example should be completed to full satisfaction and each length of metal identified most carefully as part of the master instrument. Following instruments should be matched in pitch to this example. With both tubular and bar glockenspiel, unpleasant *beats* may result from the use of instruments which are not in tune with one another.

Drill only one $\frac{5}{32}''$ hole in each piece of metal. If this hole is at a nodal point it should not affect the pitch of the note. Location at the other end is by means of panel pins which do not pass through the metal. Bicycle valve rubber sleeves on each panel pin allow full vibration but prevent unpleasant rattling. Ensure that each metal strip is supported at its nodal points. It may be necessary to adjust the near foam plastic strip to a new line if the finished lengths of metal prove to be shorter than those given in the tables. The location pins should be left as the drawing shows.

If a hand wheel-brace is used for drilling, the drill must be sharp or the aluminium will tend to clog the drill or push out into dimples instead of cutting cleanly. A pillar drill and power would make this work easy. A 'Nucleave' punch press has been used successfully for this work but the press leaves small marks on the surface of the metal. Care should be taken to preserve the smooth finish on the metal so that final polishing, before the naming of the notes with a felt pen, may be an easy task.

SPECIAL VALUE OF THE GLOCKENSPIEL. In addition to early descriptive use of the instruments and their use in exploration of note relationships by individual children, very enjoyable and profitable rhythmic exercises may be devised. Both tubular and bar instruments have separable notes and two-note, three-note and pentatonic work may be taught. The writing down of rhythms invented and the reading of existing rhythms lead naturally to the reading and recording of notes and the identification of these notes on instrument and stave. The singing quality of the sounds from these instruments appeals to children and many teachers find that a spell of singing and playing known tunes is often followed by improvisation and invention.

Sansa or Kaffir piano

Cantilever tongues of wood or metal produce the sound on this instrument. At the fixed end the tongues pass under a retaining bar and above a double bridge. All the parts are mounted on a thin board of plywood or resonant spruce. The free ends should point towards the player so that they may be plucked with the thumbs while the board is gripped with the fingers. The thickness and length of each tongue determines the note given and by adjusting the length of the projecting parts, a pentatonic or an octave diatonic scale may be made from five or eight tongues. Fine tuning adjustment may be made by tapping the ends of the tongues to shorten or lengthen the sounding portions. Examples of the instrument from Africa seldom have the tongues in order of length but for school use it may be advisable to arrange them in this order, with the long tongues to the left.

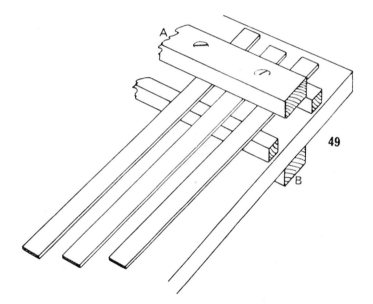

A simple sansa may be made on a board 7″ × 5″ × $\frac{3}{16}$″ with two strips of wood, one 5″ × $\frac{1}{4}$″ × $\frac{3}{16}$″ and the other the same length and width but a little thinner than $\frac{3}{16}$″. This difference in thickness between the two pieces will allow the tongues to be tilted upwards a little and will make them easier to pluck. These strips should be glued to the board 1″ apart, the outer one at a distance of 1″ from the end of the board. Five or eight tongues 6″ long and $\frac{1}{4}$″ wide should be split from odd pieces of bamboo and then planed or filed to a thickness of about $\frac{1}{8}$″. They should be thinned a little more in the middle to make them springy. Make them safe to

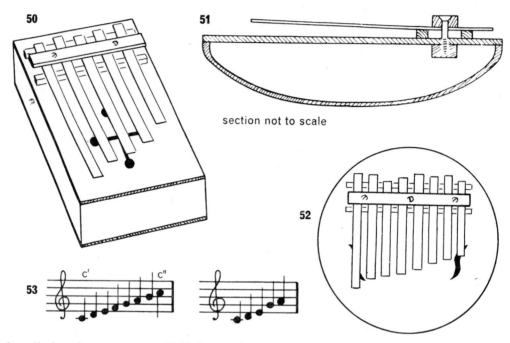

section not to scale

handle by glasspapering off all sharp edges and projections. Another lath of wood $5'' \times \frac{1}{2}'' \times \frac{5}{16}''$ will hold down these tongues if three $1''$ no. 6 countersink wood screws are passed through piece A, between the tongues and into the soundboard and a reinforcing piece B, glued to the underside. Pieces A and B are identical. See diagram 49 for the arrangement.

The notes from this simple instrument may be amplified by cutting soundholes in the board and mounting the whole on a small box as diagram 50 shows.

Diagrams 51 and 52 show how a thinly-turned bowl of beechwood may provide good amplification for tongues mounted on a board of $\frac{3}{16}''$ thickness. Soundholes should be cut in the board.

This seems to be an instrument for individual playing. Its quiet notes have little carrying power and this is part of its appeal. Shy children will sometimes retire to a corner and try various patterns on the tongues and gain confidence as tunes result from patterns. The note from a tongue is curious in that one tends to hear two notes, as with the xylophone. There is the true note which one tries to amplify, and above it a note which some people seem not to hear. This second note corresponds to the 'clang' note on the xylophone.

Bamboo tongues of the kind described will adjust easily to the notes shown in the staff notation in diagram 53. If straight-grained hardwood is used instead, tongues $\frac{3}{8}''$ wide and $\frac{1}{16}''$ thick will give about the same result.

CHAPTER THREE

Simple string instruments

THE following six instruments have been developed from older forms so that they may be made in the school workshop. Unless the instruments are used musically, only partial benefits will result from their construction in school. Their visual attraction may be sufficient to interest a group of young people in the first place and this may be followed by musical use of the items.

Each instrument consists of a strong frame which is made into a box by the addition of 4 mm plywood to the top and bottom. The frame should be of a hardwood such as utile, abura, rauli or mild mahogany; sweet chestnut has also been used. It is realised that plywood does not give such a good tone as specially chosen, resonant spruce cut 'on the quarter' but the results are lively and pleasant. By using plywood, young people are saved the difficult task of planing sound-board timber to a uniformly thin state.

The plywood should be chosen to match the frame stuff. Gaboon plywood matches some of the woods mentioned and is of the right texture and weight to give tonal response. Sen or ash plywood would match the sweet chestnut. It has been found that resin-bonded plywood of marine quality is often inert and unresponsive.

If real tonewood is available and accurate planing of thin timber is not a problem, all these instruments may be improved by using this more responsive wood for soundboards, i.e. the tables above which the strings lie. Good quality tonewood is expensive but it may be bought from suppliers of the materials for violin and guitar building. The price varies according to the quality and age. Some of the best tonewood may be obtained when an old piano is broken up. The soundboard should be extracted with as few breakages as possible but a few round holes here and there will not make the timber unusable. This timber will almost certainly be quarter-sawn and although the 'reed' (longitudinal lines made on the surface by the edges of the annual rings) may sometimes be widely spaced, the tone quality should be good. Seasoning will be no problem unless the weather has been allowed to reach the old instrument after it has been discarded.

It will be noticed that thicker pieces of timber are always used in the frames of these simple instruments where hitch and wrest pins need to be mounted. There must be sufficient substance of construction in these places to hold the pins because the combined tension of the strings is great. For glueing all parts together, Cascamite mixed at full strength has been found to be the most reliable glue. The four frame joints are pinned as well as glued but their strength lies in the glue when it has set. The pins hold the parts together until the glue has set to full strength and they are then punched just below the surface and the holes filled. This 'one-shot' glue has also the property of gap-filling and it remains moist long enough to permit normal assembly without undue drying during the process.

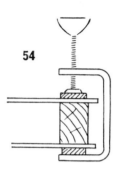

54

Tops and bottoms are *glued* to the frames and not pinned in any way. A close, flat fit is essential and great care should be taken in levelling the surfaces which meet the plywood. This is a task which needs skill with a metal jack or try plane. For cramping use (a) two full size cramping boards of $\frac{3}{4}$" multiplywood or blockboard with large G cramps or (b) many small G cramps with plywood offcut strips to protect the finished work (see diagram 54), or (c) a few small G cramps plus a set of home-made fiddle cramps. (See diagrams 55-58). Do not strain any cramps by overtightening them. Be generous with the glue and look hopefully for excess glue to ooze out along the oversize plywood margins as the cramps apply pressure.

A set of fiddle cramps

It is sometimes difficult to find a sufficient number of the small G cramps to glue the top and bottom to a frame. Fiddle cramps are easy and cheap to make. If leather washers are fitted to each cramp, there is no need to use the protective strips of plywood and hardboard when glueing is done. G cramps may then be reserved for cramping at those places where hitch and wrest pins make thicker frame stuff necessary, e.g. at the ends of the boxes.

MATERIALS REQUIRED FOR 36 CRAMPS

    3 dozen 4" no. 10 countersunk steel wood screws for the shafts

    One piece of good quality plywood $10\frac{1}{2}$" $\times$ $5\frac{1}{4}$" $\times$ $\frac{5}{8}$"

    6 dozen panel pins $\frac{1}{2}$" 18 SWG

    6 dozen tough leather washers $\frac{7}{8}$" diameter and $\frac{3}{16}$" holes

Mark on the plywood 72 squares of $\frac{7}{8}$" side as shown in diagram 55. At the mid-points of *half* the number of squares drill through the plywood quite vertically $\frac{1}{8}$" holes; these holes will engage the thread of the screws. The other 36 squares should be drilled with a $\frac{3}{16}$" drill and countersunk on one side only to take the

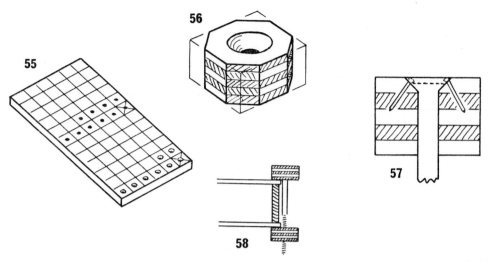

screw heads to full depth. Part off the squares from the board with a bandsaw or tenon saw and remove the corners as shown in diagram 56. Mount the large-holed octagons on the screw heads; the screw shanks should fit tightly in the holes. Two of the short panel pins driven into the ends of the saw cut, as diagram 57 shows, will enable the user to turn the screw by turning this octagon. Before screwing on the small-holed octagons, capture the washers in pairs between the top and bottom octagons.

These cramps are light in weight and easy to use. The leather pads should be kept clean and free from hard glue. The screws should not be overtightened or the internal threads will strip. It is a good idea to blunt the sharp ends of the screws to prevent injury to the hands. In glueing on tops and bottoms it is important not to have too great an amount of spare plywood overhanging the frames or the cramps will tighten down on two thicknesses of plywood with nothing between and the plywood will be distorted. Look at diagram 58 for the correct usage.

FINISH OF THE BASIC BOXES. Cleaning consists of the removal of excess plywood and glue and scraping and glasspapering to cabinet standard. An isolated extra arrow appears on some of the drawings at the corners of the boxes; this indicates the direction in which the smoothing plane should be used to clean the end grain at this point. End grain is more difficult to plane than other surfaces and the plane used should be finely sharpened and set. The lyre in particular needs special care in this matter and the arrow directions should be noted.

Bridges should be glued on before varnishing the box. Two coats of carefully applied Valspar varnish have been found satisfactory and Ronseal also gives a good finish without adding too much weight to the resonant surfaces. Ronseal usually needs three thin coats but they are easy to apply with a small cloth instead of a brush. Care should be taken not to apply any of the finishes thickly because of the deadening effect of thick varnish; treat the first coat as a sealer and do not expect a shine from it. If a shellac finish is preferred, orange flake shellac in spirit may be rubbed on with a pad. Try to avoid giving such an instrument a dreary shellac look by using this material only when the colour of the timber is fairly dark. Shellac will not spoil the looks of a dark timber but on light coloured wood clear Ronseal is better.

FITTINGS. The strings are of metal, either in the form of piano wire or as plectrum guitar strings, some of which are 'covered' to increase the weight of the string. Only metal strings are likely to remain in tune for reasonable periods. The tensioning of the strings is by *short zither wrest pins* turned by a square socket tuning key. The wrest pins are similar to the larger ones found in the wrest plank of a piano. Examine the shank of a wrest pin with a magnifying glass: one finds a shallow multi-start right hand thread. When this rudimentary screw is forced into a hole slightly smaller than the diameter of the metal, the thread grips the walls of the hole. Turning clockwise will always drive the wrest pin deeper into the hole. Spinets, harpsichords, virginals and clavichords use this size of wrest pin and sometimes longer ones of the same diameter. It follows that stringing experience gained on simple instruments is good training for later work on more advanced instruments. It ought to be mentioned that left hand wrest pins are available for special positions but that those in normal supply have right hand threads.

Commercial wrest pins are usually plated and they resist rust and discoloration. Substitutes may be made in the school workshop but they soon look shabby unless plating can be arranged. Some $\frac{3}{16}''$ bright mild steel rod should be used as stock and the square taper head filed to fit the tuning key socket. The suggestion of a thread at the other end may be made by chucking each pin in a lathe and using the ground end of a rough flat file as a hand chaser. This should be efficient enough to displace a little of the metal and make a series of thread-like burrs which will enable the shank to grip the wood. Brass would look better than steel but the square head would probably wear in use and become inefficient. Wrest pins taken from an old piano are usually of such large diameter that they are not suitable for use on these small string instruments.

The word 'wrest' is interesting. It means 'twist' or 'turn', and the word 'wrestler' springs from the same Old English root. The tuning key used to be known as the 'wrest'. In some quarters it is now known as the 'tuning hammer' because the cross bar of the T shape is sometimes used as a hammer for driving in new wrest pins. A pin is hammered in part way and finished to depth with the turning of the key.

The *hitch pins* are the anchoring devices at the loop ends of the strings. No pins less in diameter than 16 SWG are suitable for this work and it would be even safer to use 15 SWG. Remember that with the Imperial Standard Wire Gauge the thickness decreases as the gauge number increases. Most of the diagrams show the hitch pins inserted out of the vertical so that they resemble tent-pegs in their resistance to string tension. This sloping attitude seems to be worth the extra trouble that it necessitates *but do not exaggerate the slope*. Pre-boring with a $\frac{1}{16}''$ drill is also worth the extra effort. These holes need not be bored to full depth. Note that it is a coincidence that a $\frac{1}{16}''$ drill is recommended for drilling a hole for a hitch pin of 16 SWG. There is no connection between the numbers. The pins should be entered and driven in *singly* by hammer. It is important to drive them in so that only sufficient head protrudes for the string loop to engage: otherwise the string tension will bend the pin. Pins should never be knocked in further whilst their corresponding strings are in tension; they are certain to bend as the hammering is done. A hitch pin once bent will usually continue to bend and is better replaced with a straight one. The withdrawal of a hitch pin may mark the surface of the instrument unless a flat metal sheet is used under the pincers. Where there is room, pins are staggered a little so that the risk of splitting the wood along the grain is reduced. Screws are suggested as alternatives to the 16 SWG panel pins. Bradawl holes in hardwood are inadequate and preboring is essential for each screw. Use a $\frac{3}{32}''$ drill to the full $\frac{3}{4}''$ depth or the screw may shear off on being driven in.

Only the bowed psaltery has location pins on the bridge. It is found that the strings usually bed themselves in sufficiently where they cross the bridge or the nut. They retain their positions without losing much tension after the first few days of settling down. It is important to have the nut and bridge made of close-grained hardwood so that undue bedding down of the strings will not take place. Suitable woods are sycamore, maple, beech and cherry. Care should be taken to make a close fit between the underside of the bridge and the surface of the sound-board so that full transmission of vibrations may be made from the strings to the soundboard.

In stringing all the instruments except the bowed psaltery, the strings should not be tuned to the correct notes until all have been mounted in a barely tense state. Then the whole set should be arranged in orderly fashion, either parallel as the drawing shows, or in radiating lines, each line as straight as possible. Only then should the strings be brought to full tension by tuning carefully to pitch. Overtightening a string well beyond the note to which it should be tuned may stretch the wire, break it or bend the hitch pin. A bent hitch pin will usually continue to bend slowly. Remember that the string must pass around the wrest pin in a clockwise direction. About 3″ should normally be enough to allow for the coils which should capture the string end but 2″ is enough for the coils on a no. 5 or no. 6 plectrum guitar string. Bend down the end with the blunt end of a pencil but do not let this leg be long enough to reach and score the wood when the pin is turned. Next, press the string with the finger against the pin at point x to help it to hug the metal. There will then be two rightangle bends which will help to control the wire as the tuning key begins to wind the slack on the wrest pin. Turn the pin with the key and guide the slack with the left hand so that the first turn captures the short leg which has already been bent down. Diagram 59 helps to show these points.

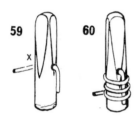

Diagram 60 shows how the coils should be arranged neatly, each succeeding coil descending the pin. Kinks should be avoided. Always practise on the thinnest string in a group because piano wire resists control and some of the thicker strings are of fighting strength. The wire is of high tensile steel but it may be cut easily with side-cutting pliers. Unfortunately, the cut ends resemble miniature chisels and they will penetrate the thickest human skin. A deep prick from a harmless-looking end of music wire is painful and one learns to treat the wire with great care. *No instrument should be accounted finished until every end of wire is held down on its wrest pin and the instrument is free from protruding dangers to people who handle it.* The safest procedure is for two people to string an instrument, one to manipulate the tools and materials, the other to hold down the box and place holding fingers as directed. See plate 5.

A simple psaltery

Pictures and carvings from the Middle Ages show us psalteries which vary in shape from triangular and trapezoid to 'pig's snout'. Diagram 61 shows some of these shapes. The gradual reduction in length of the strings from bass to treble helped to determine these functional shapes.

For ease of construction the simple psaltery, described here and drawn full-size on the loose sheet of drawings, has been made rectangular. The variation in string length has been achieved by using a sloping bridge. The stringing may be either pentatonic or one-octave diatonic. Although the instrument is small, the string

61 psalteries of traditional shape

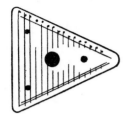 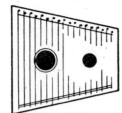 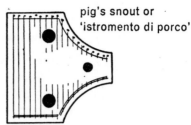

pig's snout or
'istromento di porco'

tension is great and the box will be strong enough to withstand this tension only
if the workmanship is good and the glueing effective.

MATERIALS REQUIRED

8 short zither wrest pins (or 6 for the pentatonic version), r.h. thread
1 tuning key
8 panel pins 1″ no. 16 SWG for hitch pins OR ¾″ no. 5 raised or round head
wood screws.
12 panel pins ¾″ no. 18 SWG for the corner joints
Music wire, gauges 6, 7 and 8. A one-ounce coil of each will string many
psalteries.
2 pieces utile $11\frac{5}{8}″ \times 1\frac{3}{4}″ \times \frac{3}{8}″$ ⎫
2 pieces utile $4\frac{11}{16}″ \times 1\frac{3}{4}″ \times \frac{7}{8}″$ ⎬ Finished sizes
2 pieces gaboon plywood $12\frac{1}{4}″ \times 4\frac{7}{8}″ \times 4$ mm
1 piece sycamore $7″ \times \frac{1}{2}″ \times \frac{1}{2}″$ ready to plane to section
Cascamite glue
2 cramping boards of ¾″ plywood or blockboard, $12\frac{1}{2}″ \times 5″$.

Make the frame of the box with snug, well-fitting joints. Assemble dry to check
for good fit and freedom from wind and then glue and pin the joints, using a stout
mix of Cascamite to wet all meeting surfaces. When the glue is set, punch the pin
heads just below the surface and then true top and bottom faces with a finely-set
metal smoothing plane. Check for complete flatness and freedom from wind so
that good contact with the top and bottom plywood is certain. Cut the $1\frac{1}{4}″$ hole
in the soundboard. Cover generously the top and bottom faces of the frame with
stout Cascamite, position the plywood pieces carefully and cramp the whole as
soon as possible. This box is small enough to be cramped in a nipping press. If no
press is available, use cramping boards or small G cramps and fiddle cramps.

Allow the glue to set and then remove excess plywood and glue. Clean the box
to cabinet standard. Mark lightly in pencil the position of the bridge. Plane the
bridge stuff to the section shown and ensure that the bottom face is true so that

good contact with the soundboard may be made. A planing jig will be needed

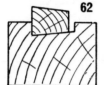

62 for planing the bevels; leave the ends of the sycamore square so that the wood will stay in the jig when the plane cuts. A cross-section of the jig or cradle is shown in diagram 62. The diagram does not show that each end has a stop to prevent the wood from sliding out.

Cut the bridge to length and glue it in place with a weight to hold it down. Varnish the whole box and then make templates for hitch and wrest pin positions. Mark these positions lightly on the ends of the soundboard. The wrest pins may appear to be out of line with the hitch pins but this is because the strings pass *around* the hitch pins. To save the necessity of forming loops in the music wire, a single length of wire is used for each pair of strings. Position the wire on each pair of hitch pins before engaging the free ends on the wrest pins. Take note of all that has been written about stringing in the preliminary to this section. One realises that it is not an ideal arrangement to allow a string to speak between a bridge and a wrest pin, without nut in between; the nut has been omitted for ease of making. If the height of the strings at the wrest pin end is kept uniformly low, children learn quickly to find the strings and play without plucking too hard.

TUNING OF THE SIMPLE PSALTERY. A basic scale of D is shown but C may be used from the beginning instead of D. A well-fitting tuning key is needed because the amount of turn needed to alter a note is slight. This is because the string

63 with six strings

sounding d'''

sounding written

with eight strings

sounding written

64a 'Past Three o'clock'. For the pentatonic psaltery in the tuning related to key **G**. Counting the shortest string as the first, begin to play on the fourth. The only note outside the compass is (e‴).

tension is great. The other five string instruments are easier to tune. Minor scales may also be used with the eight-note psaltery.

The psaltery should be held or placed so that the lowest–pitched string is nearest the body. The middle of the string should be plucked gently with the finger tip. The finger nail should not touch the string.

The ultimate value of these string instruments is in ensemble but they provide similar experiences to those which the glockenspiel and xylophone provide, i.e. descriptive and imitative sounds, background and effects for mime and drama, exploration of note relationships and scales, improvisation and invention, work in reading notes from the stave and the reverse process of recording on paper what has been played. The notes are not freely separable as they were in the glockenspiel and the resonated xylophone, but the unwanted notes in a tune may be blanked off by hanging on the strings v pieces of stiff paper folded lengthwise from rectangles 2″ × ¾″. These papers may be regarded as indicators for the unwanted notes rather than as dampers.

64b 'Barbara Allen'. Begin to play on the eighth string, the longest. For the diatonic psaltery in D major.

An enjoyable exercise is to institute a search for tunes which will fit within the octave provided by the eight notes or within the five plus the octave note of the pentatonic psaltery. The children concerned need to have a repertoire of tunes to be able to do this.

Two tunes are given so that a completed instrument may be tried immediately. In playing 'Past three o'clock' in ensemble, the phrase containing the e''' would be given to another instrument. Another tune suitable for this pentatonic tuning is the 'Skye Boat Song'. Other tunes suitable for the octave psaltery are 'There was an old woman' (doh to doh'), 'This old Man' (doh to lah) and the first part of 'Oranges and Lemons' (doh to soh).

One-octave and two-octave zithers

These are unfretted instruments rather like the psaltery. The smaller one isolates a diatonic scale an octave lower in pitch than that of the rectangular psaltery. The larger instrument contains this same octave within a compass of two octaves. Full-size drawings are given at the end of the book.

MATERIALS REQUIRED

One-octave zither	*Two-octave zither*
1 tuning key	1 tuning key
8 short zither wrest pins	15 ditto, r.h. thread
8 panel pins 1″ no. 16 SWG (hitch pins) OR $\frac{3}{4}$″ no. 5 raised or round head wood screws	15 ditto
12 panel pins $\frac{3}{4}$″ no. 18 SWG (for joints)	12 ditto
Music wire, gauges 6, 7, 8 and 9	MWG 4, 5, 6, 7, 8 and 9
Side: 1 piece utile $21\frac{1}{8}$″ × $1\frac{3}{16}$″ × $\frac{3}{8}$″	1 piece $23\frac{9}{16}$″ × $1\frac{3}{16}$″ × $\frac{3}{8}$″
Side: 1 piece utile $14\frac{1}{16}$″ × $1\frac{3}{16}$″ × $\frac{3}{8}$″	1 piece $10\frac{7}{8}$″ × $1\frac{3}{16}$″ × $\frac{3}{8}$″

Short end: 1 piece utile $4\frac{1}{2}'' \times 1\frac{3}{16}'' \times \frac{7}{8}''$ 1 piece $7\frac{3}{4}'' \times 1\frac{3}{16}'' \times \frac{7}{8}''$

Sloping end: 1 piece utile $11'' \times 1\frac{3}{16}'' \times 1\frac{1}{8}''$ 1 piece $18'' \times 1\frac{3}{16}'' \times 1\frac{1}{8}''$

1 piece gaboon 3 plywood $39'' \times 4\frac{5}{8}'' \times 4$ mm   1 piece $38'' \times 7\frac{7}{8}'' \times 4$ mm

Nut: 1 piece sycamore $4\frac{1}{2}'' \times \frac{7}{8}'' \times \frac{1}{4}''$ 1 piece $7\frac{3}{4}'' \times \frac{7}{8}'' \times \frac{1}{4}''$

Bridge: 1 piece sycamore $10\frac{1}{2}'' \times \frac{1}{2}'' \times \frac{1}{4}''$ 1 piece $17'' \times \frac{1}{2}'' \times \frac{1}{4}''$

Brass countersunk wood screws, 3, $1'' \times 6$ 5, $1'' \times 6$

2 cramping boards slightly oversize, of $\frac{3}{4}''$ plywood or blockboard   2 cramping boards slightly oversize, of $\frac{3}{4}''$ plywood or blockboard

Brass, iron or steel wire, 14 or 16 SWG for the nut pressure bar over which the strings bend at right angles

1 piece $4\frac{1}{2}''$ long   1 piece $7\frac{3}{4}''$ long

Each rectangle of plywood will cut into a top and a bottom for one instrument but the shapes required are better marked out by glueing and pinning the frame together and then using this as a template on the plywood.

The construction of the square end is the same as that of the octave psaltery. The other end has a more difficult joint because of the angles involved, but careful marking out and sawing to the lines should give snug joints. Mr. Kenneth Ansell of Selwood School, Frome, where this instrument was first adopted as part of a secondary school project, has made the suggestion that the end piece should be 'fabricated' from two pieces and the corresponding joints modified. Diagram 65 shows how the two pieces may be glued together after the ends have been shot with a plane to the correct angles. A small *jig* or shooting device should be made for this shooting process and the wood held to the jig with a G cramp. See diagram 65a.

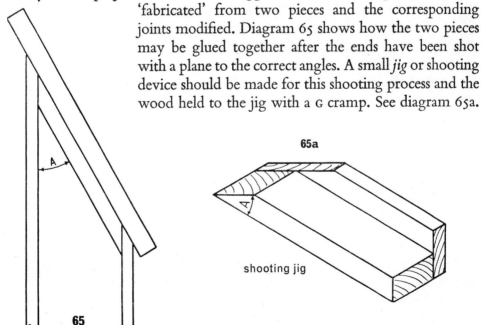

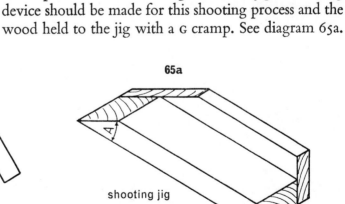

65a

shooting jig

65

In glueing the frame it may be found difficult to retain the parallel between the sides. Temporary braces of lath may be pinned across from side to side to hold the shape until the glue has set. Edge-facing, glueing and cleaning follow the same order as for the octave psaltery. Note the arrow directions for end-grain planing.

The nut should not be planed to its trapezoid section until it is glued in place. It should be fitted carefully and glued only with Cascamite of full strength. The strain on this piece of wood is two-directional and the strings tend to drag it towards the bridge. In such a position some modern glues will 'stretch'. Cramp the nut carefully in place and level the ends with the box after the glue has set. Plane the upper surface of the nut to the bevel shown and with a cutting gauge take off the small rebate to accommodate the protecting wire. This wire should stand proud of the upper surface of the nut so that the strings do not touch wood as they leave the nut towards the bridge. Finally, reinforce the attachment of the nut to the box with the 1″ countersunk screws.

Fit the bridge carefully and glue it in place. The bevels may be planed before or after the glueing. For planing after glueing, lay a thickness of card on the sound-board to protect the surface against accidental marking by the plane.

Varnish the whole and leave to dry before marking the positions of wrest and hitch pins. Two templates should be made and the exact positions marked on the box. Note that hitch pins 1 and 15 of the two-octave instrument, and 1 and 8 of the one-octave, are off-set so that they do not penetrate the joints of the frame. All hitch pins have a slight cant and are staggered so that splitting of the end block is less likely. The wrest pins are not staggered because they are more widely spaced. The holes for the latter should be drilled with a no. 13 gauge or a 4.5 mm drill to the depth of the threaded portion.

Mount the strings in pairs from the thinnest to the thickest, so that the more manageable wire is used first. The last string of the two-octave instrument is single instead of one of a pair and the end of this should be laced around hitch pins 13 and 14 in addition to 15, before the 13/14 pair is mounted. This lacing will be enough to secure the loose end. The rebate wire on the nut will be held in place by pressure from the strings. Before tuning the instrument, arrange the strings in parallel and equidistant lines.

TUNING. The main scale in diagram 66 is from d′ to d″ in D major. There are notes down to a low soh and notes up to a high soh. This main scale may be tuned instead to C major or E major and the extra seven notes accordingly. If A major is needed, it is easy to achieve by counting the a, a′ and a″ as tonic and sharpening the g′ and the g″. Other small changes will give minor scales.

66 notes of the two-octave zither

sounding and written

(compass of the .
one-octave zither)

A tune to play when a one-octave zither is completed:

67 'London Bridge'.   Counting the shortest string as the first, begin to play on the fourth.

The melodies suggested for the octave psaltery are suitable also for this octave zither. Others are 'The First Nowell' (doh to doh'), 'Here's to the maiden of bashful fifteen' (doh to doh') and the first four lines of 'Oranges and Lemons' (doh to soh).

All the melodies suitable for the one-octave instrument may be played on the two-octave version, and in addition, many melodies which need a few notes outside the octave. 'In dulci jubilo' (lah, to lah) is an example. However, when a low lah or a low soh occurs in a melody, this note in the key of D major may be too low for the singers. If a choir is to sing the song or carol, the key of the melody must be determined by the compass of the voices and it may be possible to use the instrument in its A major tuning. For example, a song like 'O Soldier, Soldier' (me, to soh) would then run from c'$^\sharp$ to e''.

The two-octave zither is also useful in providing plucked fifths in the same kind of accompaniment as that suggested for the xylophones.

The Nordic lyre

This is based on the Finnish *Kantele* and has a two-octave diatonic scale rising from the D below middle C. Most of the strings are covered steel.

MATERIALS REQUIRED

    1 tuning key

    15 short zither wrest pins, r.h. thread

    15 panel pins 1" no. 16 SWG for hitch pins OR $\frac{3}{4}$" no. 5 raised or round head wood screws

    12 panel pins $\frac{3}{4}$" no. 18 SWG for frame joints

    1 piece utile $13\frac{1}{2}$" × $1\frac{1}{4}$" × $\frac{3}{8}$"   ⎫

    1 piece utile $21\frac{3}{4}$" × $1\frac{1}{4}$" × $\frac{3}{8}$"   ⎬ Sizes planed to width and thickness

    2 pieces utile $1\frac{1}{4}$" thick, sawn to shapes for end blocks

    2 pieces 4 mm gaboon 3 plywood cut slightly oversize to shape of frame

    1 piece sycamore $16\frac{1}{2}$" × $\frac{7}{16}$" × $\frac{7}{16}$" (bridge) ⎫ Planed sizes before bevels are

    1 piece sycamore 6" × $\frac{7}{16}$" × $\frac{7}{16}$" (nut)   ⎬ planed

    2 cramping boards slightly oversize, of $\frac{3}{4}$" plywood or blockboard

    Plectrum guitar strings, loop-ended (Toggle-ended strings are more difficult

        B (no. 2) 3   to attach to the hitch pins).

        G (no. 3) 5

        D (no. 4) 3

        A (no. 5) 4

  Total strings 15

Two accurate templates must be cut for the end block and the curved arm These templates should incorporate the drilling points which will be needed later for the hitch and wrest pins. Joints to be hand cut will need careful marking and squaring across the edges. If a bandsaw is used, there will be little need for subsequent adjustment. Check the assembled but unglued frame against the drawing and ensure that the joints fit before glueing and pinning. The use of a vice is essential for pinning with the $\frac{3}{4}$" no. 18 panel pins. Compared with a rectangular frame, this unusual shape is difficult to check for flatness and freedom from wind. Careful scrutiny must be made before top and bottom are glued in place.

A wood file or carbide cintride file in addition to scraper and glasspaper will help in the cleaning of the box edges after the initial planing has been done.

The nut and bridge should fit accurately against the soundboard. Glue both in place and weight down with two try planes until the glue has set. Trim off the ends level with the edges of the box and take care not to mark the box with the saw.

After varnishing, insert the pins in the usual way and mount the first string, a no. 2 plectrum guitar string. The loop simply needs to be slipped over the hitch pin, which should protrude sufficiently (but no more) for the loop to engage. The free end should be cut with 3″ to spare and coiled on the wrest pin. By the time the no. 5 strings are used, it will be seen that rather less than 3″ is enough for the coils because these thicker strings take up more space on the wrest pins. In spite of the large size of this instrument, stringing takes less time than on any other of the instruments because the hitching loops are already formed.

TUNING. Other slight variations may be made but strings should not normally be tuned to notes more than a tone below or a tone above their usual pitch.

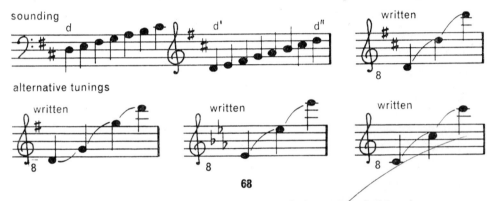

A MELODY TO PLAY. This will be an octave below the children's voices.

69 'Unto us a child is born'. Begin to play on the longest string.

Bowed psaltery

The details of this version of the 'Streichpsalter' are given by permission of Professor Edgar Stahmer who has been using the instrument in schools in Germany for some years. The unusual arrangement of strings allows the end portion of each string to be bowed. The scale is chromatic. The box materials and the wire cost very little and the main expense is that of the wrest pins; 48 are needed. Expense may be reduced by using for the 24 *fixed* pins short lengths of $\frac{3}{16}''$ mild steel or brass rod. Lateral holes may be drilled through each length for the string to pass through. The top of each short rod should be given a filed nick. This same operation is necessary if short zither wrest pins are used for the fixed pins. The nick carries the wire over the top and retains it in that position. These fixed pins do not need the shallow thread because they are not used for tuning. The tuning pins are mounted in a closely-spaced group on the short side of the isosceles triangle.

MATERIALS REQUIRED

    1 tuning key
    48 short zither wrest pins, r.h. thread
    2 pieces utile $22\frac{1}{2}'' \times 1'' \times \frac{13}{16}''$ } Sizes planed to width and thickness
    1 piece utile $8'' \times 1\frac{3}{16}'' \times 1''$
    4 mm gaboon plywood to cover top and bottom and cut slightly oversize
    1 piece sycamore $5\frac{1}{2}'' \times \frac{7}{16}'' \times \frac{7}{16}''$ (This is slightly oversize).
    24 panel pins $\frac{1}{2}''$ no. 18 SWG for location pins on the bridge
    Gauge 0 music wire
    1 piece split bamboo $20'' \times \frac{1}{2}'' \times \frac{1}{8}''$
    Bow hair—about 80 strands washed and combed
    Rosin, sealing wax, fine thread
    2 cramping boards slightly oversize, of $\frac{3}{4}''$ plywood or blockboard

These timber sizes are given in inches but the full size drawing will be found dimensioned in millimetres.

The corner joints may be halved as shown, or mitred, glued and pinned. If halved joints are to be made, assemble the planed wood in a triangle of the exact size shown on the drawing. Overlap the pieces at the corners and grip the overlaps with three small G cramps until the shoulder lines have been marked out, one piece from another. Scribe a line wherever a shoulder needs to be cut. Release the cramps and gauge the halvings from a common surface with a gauge setting of half the 1″ dimension. Join shoulder lines to gauge lines with verticals. Saw these barefaced tenons to their skew shoulders and release the waste by sawing to the shoulder lines. Fit carefully, assemble dry with three small G cramps and check the joints for a good fit. The triangle should be of exact size with the drawing. Glue and cramp, using stout Cascamite.

If mitre joints are used instead of halvings, three settings of the sliding bevel will be needed because of the difference of stuff dimensions.

When the frame is glued and the glue is set, level top and bottom faces carefully with a try plane. Cut the hole in the soundboard, glue the box together and allow the glue to set. Clean up carefully, and round off the corners as the drawing suggests.

The bridge should finish at 1 cm × 1 cm in section before the bevels are planed. Hold the sycamore in a jig to plane the bevels and finish the surfaces by rubbing the wood *on* a flat sheet of no. 1 glasspaper. Drill the entry holes for the location pins with a $\frac{1}{32}''$ drill so that the bridge will not split when the pins are driven in. The insertion of the pins may be made after the bridge has been glued exactly in place on the soundboard.

Varnish the box before marking out the positions of the 48 wrest pins. Two precise templates must be used for these positions. With the closely spaced group of 24 tuning pins it is essential to be accurate; if any one of these pins is out of place it may be found that the tuning key will not engage the pin because the key fouls the next pin in the group. Drill all the holes with a no. 13 gauge or a 4.5 mm drill to the depth of the thread but insert only the stationary pins which lie along the equal sides of the triangle. Line up the tops by casting an eye along each row and adjusting so that all stand equal in height above the soundboard. Make the string holes face fore and aft, at right angles to the bridge. Use a small saw file of triangular section for filing the groove on each tip. This groove should be in line with the string hole and need not be deep. Cut it with the file in the right hand and, with the thumb and first finger of the left hand, locate the file in position on the tip of the pin.

Of the tuning pins, insert only the two outer pins on each side. It will be found easier to insert these pins one by one as the corresponding strings are mounted. Study the path of the shortest string on the drawing; it begins as a short leg at the inner end of the string hole on the fixed pin, passes through the hole and returns on the outside of the pin to capture the short leg with about three coils of string. Then it returns through the hole in its original direction and climbs the outside of the pin to lie in its groove on the tip. If the wire is taken along this route without leaving too much slack, it may be held temporarily with a $1\frac{1}{2}''$ length of Sellotape while the other end of the wire is dealt with. Allow the first string to be deflected by the first positioning pin on the bridge and leave about 3″ of wire at the end to make a few coils on the tuning pin. Mount this end of the string in the normal way on the wrest pin and finally tune the string to g‴. Insert the tuning pins in turn and mount the corresponding strings. When all the naturals have been mounted, the f‴♯ on the other side may be strung and tuned. Note the new path around the end positioning pin for this string and the change-over for these paths at about point x on the drawing. Final tuning should be made when all the strings have been mounted. This instrument should remain well in tune when the assembly has settled down.

The bow

The piece of split bamboo should be planed and glasspapered to remove sharp edges. It should form a springy lath and at each end a slot ½″ long and a bare ⅛″ wide should be cut for the hair. With fine thread tie one end of each strand into a fine bunch and dip these ends in molten sealing wax to form a small ball or plug which cannot pass the ⅛″ slot. Dampen, comb and straighten the switch before making a similar ball at the other end. Allow a stick deflection of about 2″ from the straight when the bent stick puts the hair in tension. When the hair is dry it must be dressed with rosin.

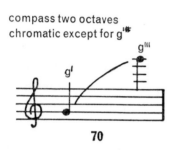

compass two octaves
chromatic except for g′♯

70

TUNING AND PLAYING THE BOWED PSALTERY. The notes to which the strings should be tuned are given on the full size drawing on the inserted sheet. See also diagram 70 for the compass of the instrument. Tune the notes of the strings to the notes of a piano. In playing, rest the short side of the triangle against the body just above the left hip, and with the left hand, support the instrument towards the other end. Holding the bow in the right hand, bow the far end of each string. See plate 6. The diatonic scale of C is on the right. Reach over to the other side for the sharps and flats. It is necessary to lift the bow from string to string. True legato playing is impossible but it is easy to play sustained notes, and these are particularly acceptable when used with tuned percussion instruments.

PLAYING IN C MAJOR. 'Little brown jug' in diagram 71a is rather a fast tune but all the notes lie conveniently along one side of the triangle. The points at which to bow the two C strings may be marked with chalk or stamp edging on the soundboard underneath the strings. If the G also is marked, there should be little difficulty in identifying the notes of the melody. An even pressure of the bow at right angles to the string line will give the best tone. Attempts should be made to sustain notes for their maximum time values by using as much of the bow hair as possible.

PLAYING IN G MAJOR. The example in 64a, 'Past three o'clock', may be used as

71a 'Little Brown Jug'

71b 'All through the night'

an easy introduction to this key because it does not involve the F sharp. This melody is also slower than that in diagram 71a and the bowing need not be hurried. 'All through the night' in diagram 71b involves the F sharp from the beginning but the repetition is a valuable feature. The AABA pattern of the melody will be noted.

Another useful tune in G major is 'O no John'. This uses F sharp twice only. 'The Birds', a Czech carol from the Oxford Book of Carols may be tried. When this melody is played in G major it calls for F sharp. In addition it needs C sharp as an accidental.

A MELODY IN G MINOR. In the Coventry Carol in G minor the familiar F sharp will be found as an accidental. The B flat is the only new note if the other examples have been tried. This B flat is changed to B natural in the last two bars.

Chordal dulcimer

This is the only non-melodic instrument in this group of simple strings. It is strictly not a dulcimer but the name grew out of an attempt to describe the instrument to other people as the variety of these simple instruments for schools grew. A larger instrument of this type may be seen in the Horniman Museum. This came from the Basque country and it is known as the *tambourin*. In construction, the chordal dulcimer box is an enlargement of the one-octave psaltery box but it is provided with two bridges instead of one. There is nothing new in the making of the box if the details of the psaltery box are familiar.

MATERIALS REQUIRED

1 tuning key

12 short zither wrest pins, r.h. thread

12 panel pins 1″ no. 16 SWG OR $\frac{3}{4}$″ no. 5 raised or round head wood screws

12 panel pins $\frac{3}{4}$″ no. 18 SWG for the corner joints

2 pieces utile 8$\frac{1}{4}$″ ×2″ ×$\frac{7}{8}$″ ⎫ Finished sizes

2 pieces utile 24$\frac{3}{8}$″ ×2″ ×$\frac{3}{8}$″ ⎭

2 pieces gaboon plywood 25″ ×8$\frac{3}{8}$″ ×4 mm

2 pieces sycamore 8$\frac{1}{2}$″ ×$\frac{7}{16}$″ ×$\frac{7}{16}$″ ready to plane to section

1 piece hardwood 10$\frac{1}{4}$″ ×1″ ×$\frac{1}{2}$″ for the beater

1 piece thick, close felt 1$\frac{1}{2}$″ ×1$\frac{1}{4}$″ from an old hat

2 cramping boards of $\frac{3}{4}$″ plywood or block-board, 25″ × 8$\frac{1}{2}$″

Plectrum guitar strings, loop-ended:

B (no. 2)		1
G (no. 3)		3
D (no. 4)		5
A (no. 5)		2
E (no. 6)		1
		—
Total strings		12
		—

Make up the box and plane the two bridges to the section shown on the drawing. Glue the two bridges in place and varnish. Mark the pin positions from an accurate template and drill the wrest pin holes with a no. 13 gauge or a 4.5 mm drill. The hitch pins are tilted slightly and the $\frac{1}{16}$" holes should be drilled at the angle shown on the drawing in the sectional elevation; this angle should not be exaggerated.

Stringing is easy. The only delay may occur when the cut end of the no. 6 string is offered to the appropriate string hole in the wrest pin. This hole may need enlargement, and careful drilling with a $\frac{1}{16}$" drill in a wheel brace should clear the hole. Take care not to break the drill in this hole; the metal of the drill may be more brittle than one expects. Keep carefully to the arrangement of strings shown on the drawing. Various arrangements have been tried but there are decided advantages in having chord I near the body and II, V and IV next in order.

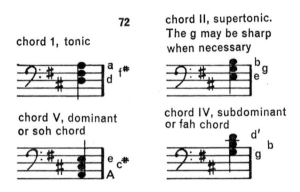

72

chord 1, tonic

chord II, supertonic. The g may be sharp when necessary

chord V, dominant or soh chord

chord IV, subdominant or fah chord

TUNING. The tunings are given for a tonic chord of D major but the basis may be C or E major (or keys between) without changing any of the strings. Like the other string instruments, the chordal dulcimer holds pitch better if a basic tuning is decided upon and only small variations are made to suit the accompaniments to be played.

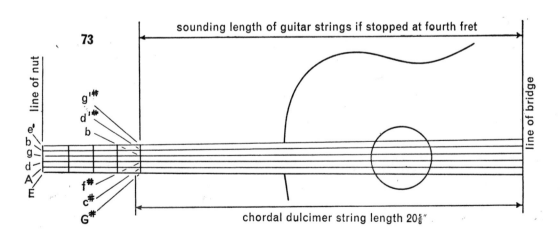

73

line of nut

line of bridge

sounding length of guitar strings if stopped at fourth fret

chordal dulcimer string length $20\frac{5}{8}$"

If a completely different chordal structure is considered, strings to suit the notes needed must be chosen on the basis of the plectrum guitar string length of $25\frac{1}{2}''$ for each open string note e′ b g d A and E. The chordal dulcimer string length of $20\frac{5}{8}''$ must be laid against this $25\frac{1}{2}''$ and compared with a guitar fingerboard. From this fingerboard may be found the appropriate string for a given note. Look at diagram 73. By choosing the string which is nearest in pitch, at this point, to the pitch required, it will be certain that the chosen string will be in approximately correct tension when it is used.

THE BEATER. Cut this to a graceful shape that gives good balance in the hand. Only one side of the spade end should be covered with felt. Two effects may be obtained by striking, one with and the other without the use of the felt; one sound gives a contrast to the other but the felt side will be used more than the plain. The felt should not be thicker than $\frac{1}{16}''$ or $\frac{3}{32}''$ or the sounds will be muted.

USE OF THE CHORDAL DULCIMER BY THE TEACHER. When the instrument is the only one to accompany a song, one finds that the beater is used less as playing skill grows and the accompaniments become more selective. Two notes and even single notes here and there are often more acceptable than triads. For this type of work, plucking is necessary and the hands should find suitable resting places where the strings are easy to find by feel alone.

USE OF THE CHORDAL DULCIMER BY CHILDREN. The beater is needed when children begin to use the instrument in providing pulse and harmony at their simplest, and join other children who may be playing melodic instruments. Those tunes which need only chords I and V give a good starting point, especially those which change from I to V at the beginning of a new bar and hold that harmony for a bar or two. A good example of this type of tune is 'Polly Wolly Doodle'. 'Poor Mary sits aweeping' would be a good tune with which to follow, and 'When I was a young girl' and 'Sur le pont d'Avignon' are almost as easy. The next step would be the introduction of the fah chord or chord IV. Examples of the use of this are 'The muffin man', 'Jinny crack corn' and 'Early one morning'. Children who take part in this work with guidance often develop very quickly the ability to decide which chords are needed in a given tune. It is soon found that it is impossible to accompany every tune with the four chords available and much useful work may be done in classifying well-known melodies according to their harmonic basis. Recognition of the chords by their names 'doh chord', 'soh chord' or 'fah chord' should be followed by presentation and use of the chords from the stave.

CHAPTER FOUR

Materials, sources and usage

BUILDERS of professional standard musical instruments must spend time and capital in laying down and caring for stocks of material. The timber, in particular, must be well sawn or cleft. It must be well seasoned and reliable so that it will not bow or warp after work has begun. It must conform to certain traditions in the matter of appearance. Above all, the tone value must be high. The violin, viola and cello have probably the most exacting requirements. If substitute timbers are used for these instruments, a luthier may well be left with unsold instruments; they may have excellent tone but be considered ugly because, for example, the reed of the belly is too wide or there is an unusual flare or figure which disturbs the line of the reed. Nothing is too good for this class of work and one should buy the best materials one can afford. On finishing a well-made instrument a beginner has often regretted spending the time on poor material and wished that he had bought better stuff. First-hand advice from a practising luthier and close examination of many mature instruments of good standard are the best preparation. The cost of good material may surprise one at first. A very old and dirty wedge-shaped piece of maple for a violin back may change hands for eight or ten pounds but it is possible to buy a reasonably good piece for about two pounds. Twelve pounds should buy all the materials for a violin. Viola materials of good quality would cost about £15 and for a cello very much more. (The *dearest* unworked cello back in a recent timber list was £58.) The total prices quoted are for the timber and accessories such as pegs, bridge, tail-piece, purfling and strings before any work is done on them. The small parts are seldom made by the luthier; it is easier to buy them as standard items and the time saved can then be spent on the special attention that a string instrument needs.

Learn to recognise timbers built into existing instruments and to know them again when seen in the raw at the merchant's store. Try to evaluate wood tonally by suspending pieces loosely between finger and thumb and tapping at various points to hear response. Judge whether or not they would cut reasonably well with saw, plane or gouge so that shaping might be accomplished without too much strife. Some wood may even be too soft, rather than too hard, to cut well for a given purpose or shape. One should try to understand the purpose of each component of an instrument. It should be remembered that an instrument vibrates as a whole. This is particularly true of the violin family; on this instrument, any item of construction or furnishing which is not balanced with the other parts will act adversely, perhaps as an undesirable node.

Even keyboard string instruments tonally are affected by the wood from which cases and frames are made but these instruments need not cost quite so much for materials in proportion to their size. Much of the timber used is normal, carefully selected, good quality cabinet timber and only the soundboard need normally be bought from a specialist supplier. If a component is known to take up the first vibrations of a string, e.g. a bridge or soundboard, this wood must be the ideal wood for the purpose and any substitute should have the closest scrutiny before acceptance. On the other hand, the fascia or the music stand of a spinet would not need such critical choice of timber. Neither fascia nor stand should be unduly dense or heavy but might otherwise be made from any good, well-seasoned cabinet timber.

Sets of jacks for spinets have been made from the rock maple of a blitzed gymnasium floor and keyboards from blitzed shelving of suitable quality. In considering the tonal value of the case of an instrument such as the spinet, think of two unlikely extremes: first, a case made of solid ebony, second, one of balsa. One would be hard, heavy and dense, the other soft in texture and light in weight. It seems certain that neither would help the tonal value of the instrument, no matter how well the soundboard and other components had been chosen and made.

These principles are put forward because an understanding of them enables one to assess *available* materials and to make simple instruments with more success. One cannot possibly afford quarter-sawn figured maple and Balkan spruce for first essays in school instrument building but any wood selected should give the instruments a chance of achieving good tone. And in the school workshop it is not always a matter of cost but sometimes of speed or of limitations of workmanship that substitutes must be used. Perhaps the difficulty is in planing a large area of softwood to an even thickness of three or four millimetres. This difficulty is by-passed by using plywood of known quality and thickness. Plywood needs no planing and it gives a reasonable tone on these instruments which are less demanding. (See Chapter Three). The hope is that a secondary school boy, once thoroughly involved, will realise that there is usually an ideal material for a component and that he should use this better material when he has passed the stage of beginner.

SOFTWOODS USED BY THE LUTHIER AS TONEWOOD. Wood for bellies, bass bars and soundposts of the violin family comes mainly from S.E. Europe but in recent years timber of good tone value has been imported from Canada. It should be remembered that (*a*) timber nomenclature in general is often quite misleading and that timber is sometimes sold under names which bear little relation to the names of the trees which yield it. (*b*) differing soils, climates, aspects and tree spacing will yield timber of great variation from the same variety of tree.

The general description 'pine' is often given to the timber provided for bellies but examination of many samples of known quality suggests that most of it is from varieties of spruce.

Amongst the timbers available are the following:

'Spruce', 'fir', 'red fir' and 'white pine' from Switzerland, the Tyrol, the Jura, the Vosges, Jugoslavia, the Carpathians, Italy and Norway.

Sitka spruce and similar varieties from Canada. (Boatbuilders seem to use similar qualities today and some of their quarter-sawn spruce has been found suitable for spinet and clavichord soundboards.)

Western red cedar and white cedar from Canada. Edge tools used on these timbers must be very sharp and must be used lightly because the wood is so very tender. It is so easy to break off pieces instead of cutting them.

All these softwoods have been used for front tables. It goes without saying that there should be freedom from knots and resin pockets. It is also a tradition that the natural markings of the wood should conform to certain limitations. Some experts stipulate a spacing of about one millimetre for the 'reed' of a violin belly. The spacing of the annual rings which produce this reed varies according to the growth of the tree and cannot possibly be uniform. Many samples of good tonewood cannot pass this test. Tonewood must be above all free-sounding and one suspects that many suitable pieces are rejected on account of looks alone.

One cannot find tonewood in an ordinary timberyard. The trade is in the hands of specialists. The 'bûcheron spécialiste' selects standing trees and he is said to take trees from those parts of the forest which lie between certain altitudes and which grow on the southern slopes. The extraction of suitable trees from the forest is followed by careful conversion to suitable sizes and by closely-controlled seasoning. One Swiss specialist extracts *épicéa* from his area in the Bernese Oberland. His other product is shingles for roofs and walls of chalets. Both products are cleft from short billets with primitive but efficient edge tools which appear to be at least two centuries old. His knowledge of tonewood has been gained by selecting billets, submitting them to the luthiers and discussing the material after

65

it has been worked and built into musical instruments. The standard of requirements is fixed in his mind and his judgment never varies. Cleaving instead of
sawing the billets ensures that the grain runs parallel with the length of the piece
without deviation. It is an impressive sight in the loft of such a specialist where
billets of standard sizes for violin, viola, cello and bass are stacked in semi-darkness
to season slowly and naturally. One of the biggest stocks of such timber lies in a
large, well-aired shed at the Geigenbauschule at Mittenwald, Bavaria. Here may
be seen pieces for lutes, viols and guitars in addition to wood for the instruments
already mentioned.

Some luthiers prefer to use the timber from old, dismantled chalets. There has
been quite a trade in such timber for years and one has the knowledge that the
stuff is truly seasoned. Other makers say that wood of this kind is past its best.

The velocity of sound longitudinally through spruce is said to be about fifteen
times its velocity through air and this comparison gives some idea why spruce
and similar woods are chosen as soundboards and bellies. Response from a
vibrating string mounted on such a board or belly is immediate and the vibrations
travel along and across the wood very rapidly. Maximum response is produced
when the wood is 'quarter-sawn' and the cut edges of the annual growth rings
(or *reed*) appear at their narrowest on the surfaces of the soundboard, parallel
with the edges of the board and with one another. On the end grain these rings
show as verticals to the faces of the board. See diagram 74.

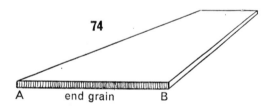

When the timber is cut in this way the shrinkage from A to B is at a minimum.
Maximum shrinkage is normally circumferential. Thus, in addition to good tone,
one obtains good stability and behaviour of the main component of the instrument. This is important when all items are so thin and glue alone holds the
instrument together. Even well-seasoned wood tends to vary in size and shape as
the moisture content of the atmosphere varies. Ideally, the moisture content of
wood used for musical instruments should be suited to the room in which each
instrument is to stay. There are many types of heating in use in buildings in the
United Kingdom; some are radiator-heated, some by warm air ducts, and some

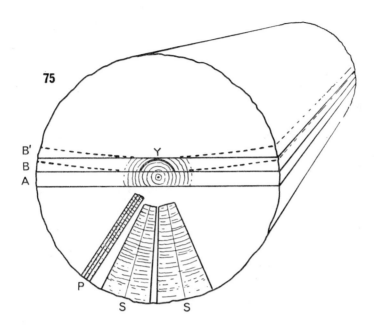

still have fires or stoves which go out at night and leave the rooms completely unheated. The moisture content of the air resulting from these types of heating must vary considerably. In many ways, moisture content is more important than temperature when the behaviour of wood is concerned. It is not surprising that piano manufacturers have found it difficult to build instruments which will withstand the variations in conditions.

Normally, the maximum width of a quarter-sawn board from a tree is only half the diameter of the trunk because the heart is seldom included in a belly or soundboard. The heart often has a pithy nature and a poor appearance and the wider spacing of the annual rings near the heart is undesirable. Look at diagram 75. Piece A includes the heart. It may be seen that piece B is not truly quarter-sawn although it is almost as wide as board A. Because of the inclusion at the middle of board B of almost half of an annual ring (indicated by the bold line Y) and several more nearly complete half-rings, this board will warp badly soon after it has been sawn from the log. Dotted lines B′ show the probable shape of B after seasoning. The ideal pieces are cut as flat boards P or as wedge-shaped billets s, 'on the quarter'. For a wide, flat soundboard for piano or harpsichord, several of these narrow, thin boards as at P are glued together edge to edge because suitable trees do not grow wide enough to provide boards more than a few inches wide. For a curved front table for a violin, a wedge-shaped billet is

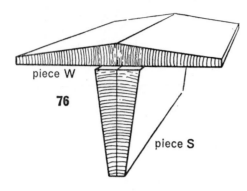

sawn or cleft and the two halves are then rejoined, broad edge to broad edge as shown in diagram 76. From this solid block w the front table may be carved. Note that this arrangement at w brings the annual rings vertical to the plane of the table. There is no disadvantage in having the belly of a violin made from two pieces if the joint is well prepared and glued. Few violins have a one-piece belly and because of the still greater width, even fewer violas and cellos. If occasionally a piece is found wide enough to make a one-piece belly it is almost certain that the spacing of the reed will be wider in that portion nearer the heart of the tree. It is usual to place this portion under the lower strings.

Special hardwoods used in instrument making

SYCAMORE and MAPLE are used for the backs, ribs, necks and scrolls of the violin family, for the viols, lutes and to a less extent for guitars. Figured wood is always chosen for professional standard work, either rippled ('fiddle-back' figure) or flamed. On old instruments one sees occasionally beech, plane, poplar and lime, but it is not worth putting good workmanship into anything but the timber specially selected for this work. Bird's eye maple is sometimes seen but this is unfashionable today and tonally suspect. Maple is durable, elastic, not too hard or heavy, and has the ability to sustain and reflect the movement transmitted to it by the ribs, the soundpost and the capacity of the box of the instrument. Sources are Bohemia, the Carpathians, Dalmatia, Jugoslavia, Hungary, Turkey and Canada. From Canada, the only common source outside south-east Europe, comes the sugar maple which has been used very successfully for string instruments. There is also a very fine-grained maple with tiny medullary ray flecks and this is made into bridges of the best kind. It seems to be unobtainable as raw material except by the specialist manufacturers. The sugar maple seems to be the nearest in texture to this timber.

No luthier would buy stock and begin to use it at once unless he had bought it from a fellow-maker who had seasoned and conditioned the wood. In a family business it is the custom to lay in stock for one's sons to use and the billets are stacked away in a well-aired but unheated loft or shed. For violin backs, the wood need not always be quarter-sawn (*sur sens* or *sur maille*). It may be slab-sawn (*sur couche*) and from a slab like that in diagram 77 a whole back may be carved. Special care in seasoning and conditioning is vital with such a slab-sawn piece. Sometimes a big sycamore tree will yield one-piece quarter-sawn backs between heart and bark but maple is nearly always converted to wedge-shaped billets because the trees are of smaller growth. Glued back joints are then needed as for the two-piece bellies.

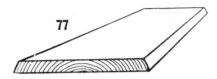

77

EBONY. Only the blackest ebony seems to be favoured for fingerboard, nut, tailpiece and, when ebony is chosen instead of rosewood, for endpin and pegs. A variety of ebony that has a black base with grey flecks has a little more character. Partly-shaped or fully-shaped fingerboards may be bought, but if unusual sizes are needed it may be necessary to buy a billet of this wood. It will be sold by weight and not by a measured size as with normal timber. Ebony pegs seem to turn very drily unless a dressing is given to the taper, whereas rosewood pegs seem to have a natural waxiness. (Flutes which appear to be made from ebony are usually of *African blackwood*, which has better tonal qualities for this purpose. 'Ebony' pianos usually have a case of pearwood or a similar wood stained black.)

BOXWOOD. Sometimes used for violin pegs, tailpiece and endpin, just occasionally for fingerboards. Good recorders have been made from it and many old flutes and clarinets combined this wood with ivory. It is sold by weight.

HONDURAS AND BRAZILIAN ROSEWOOD. Another 'very hard hardwood' used for pegs and endpins. It is less brittle than ebony and slides more easily in the peg holes as tuning is done. Also used for good-quality recorders and for the battens of some xylophones. Sold by weight.

WILLOW. Violin and guitar rib-linings are often made from this wood. Old cricket bats may be saved for a supply. This is a 'soft hardwood', light in weight, easy to bend hot to the curves needed and easy to glue to the ribs. Willow is not essential for linings and the softwood offcuts from the belly stuff may be used instead.

PERNAMBUCO. The best wood for bows; hard, heavy, dense, stiff and springy. It will take the edge off most tools in a very short time and it almost compels one to work with a blunt tool. It is also a dyewood and the shavings and sawdust may be used with alum as mordant.

BRAZILWOOD, from which cheaper bows are made commercially, is a cheaper and more plentiful wood similar to Pernambuco. Both are sold by weight.

SNAKEWOOD. Used for the best viol bows and occasionally for violin bows. Sold by weight but now rather scarce.

GREENHEART. Used occasionally for bows. The same wood is used for fishing rods.

JACARANDA (*sometimes offered as palissander*). This is not used for violins but it is a good wood for the battens of xylophones. It is not so dense and hard as Honduras rosewood. Imported in short logs and sold by weight. Read the notes about the materials for the resonated xylophone.

Other materials

PURFLING. This is the name given to the black/white/black of inlay around the edges of the front and back tables of the violin family. It seems to serve two purposes. First of all it emphasises the outline of the tables in a restrained way. Then it is considered to be a safety device which helps to prevent damage to the table edges from spreading inwards; the slight weakness of the channel edge ensures that a clean break is made. The material may be bought as a three-fold strip ready to cut to length and to be mitred at the corners. The easiest kind to use is one which has the outer blacks made from fibre. This does not snap so easily when it is bent and mitred. Various widths and styles may be bought. More elaborate inlays are available for guitar decoration.

FRET WIRE. This is brass or German silver wire of T section for inlay on the fingerboards of guitar and similar fretted instruments. It is inserted in short lengths into shallow saw kerfs across the fingerboards. Most music shops can supply this wire.

STRINGS FOR MUSICAL INSTRUMENTS. It would be possible to write a large book on strings alone. For professional-standard instruments the player often decides which strings shall be fitted. He has the choice of gut and nylon, these materials covered with fine wire, steel, steel covered with fine wire, and then the 'flexible-cored' and 'rope-cored' strings.

For the simple string instruments described in this book two main kinds are specified: (*a*) the range of steel-based plectrum guitar strings which may be obtained with loop ends; (*b*) 'music wire' which may be bought in coils.

(a) Plectrum guitar strings, loop-ended

These normally have toggle or ball ends. Strings bought from the nearest shop will be toggle-ended unless they have been ordered specially. It is not easy to cut the toggle from the loop. One breaks or cuts the loop so very easily and then the string is useless. This type of string was chosen because a covered string with a steel base has better tuning stability than most of the others.

(b) Music wire

A table of some of the sizes is given for this type of wire together with the equivalent thicknesses in thousandths of an inch. Both thicker and thinner wire is available in this gauge and in addition there are continental sizes which provide intermediates.

BRITISH MUSIC WIRE GAUGE

00	·0085″	5	·014″
0	·009″	6	·016″
1	·010″	7	·018″
2	·011″	8	·020″
3	·012″	9	·022″
4	·013″	10	·024″

CHAPTER FIVE

Activities allied with music

THESE suggestions are made for teachers who wish to interest children in sound and its production. The materials and apparatus described are usually simple and easy to find. There are three headings:

Sound from strings
Sound from moving air
Sound from rods and bars.

Sound from strings

One of the simplest ways of showing how the note from a string in tension may be amplified is by mounting a guitar string on a piece of hardwood $29'' \times 1'' \times 1''$ and tensioning the string between a wrest pin at one end and a hitch pin at the other. Two raised bars about $\frac{3}{16}''$ in height should be glued to the stick to form nut and bridge and give a sounding length of $25\frac{1}{2}''$. The string should be tuned to its nominal pitch e.g. a no. 3 string should be tuned to g.

Diagram 78 shows both ends of the string–on–a–stick. It will be found that the note, whether plucked or bowed, will be faint. Pluck or bow as loudly as possible and ask one of the children to try to make an even louder sound with the device. Ask the class to listen carefully. It may be possible to draw a line across the room, beyond which the note cannot be heard. Now take the stick and place it in turn flat and then endways on a surface such as a desk or table and sound the note again. The range of audibility will have increased because of the amplification given by the desk or table.

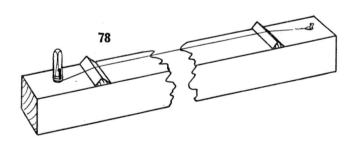

78

Other surfaces and then containers such as tins and boxes may be used with the string-on-a-stick to show that a wooden box well in contact with the stick gives the best result. The quality as well as the volume of sound will be affected so that the nasal note of the string may well be changed to a much more acceptable sound. It may be found that a box of a certain size will give the best result and this box may not be the biggest box tried. One of the slit drums may be used to attach to the stick for these experiments.

PRIMITIVE PLUCKED BASS INSTRUMENTS. A batten fixed to a tea chest and a stout cord stretched between the two may be used as a simple plucked bass. The batten should be flexed slightly to vary the tension on the cord. Intonation by this method is only approximate. See diagram 79.

The *bombass* or *vozembouch* uses a bladder to amplify notes from a string. Fit a stick or pole about 6′ × 2″ × ¾″ with a strong cord and pass the cord over a large inflated bladder (pig or football). Plucking the string produces quite far-reaching sounds. Different notes may be produced by flexing the stick slightly or by moving the left hand along the cord to alter the sounding length of the string. A picture by Johannes Steen shows this primitive instrument used in carnival mood. The player is using a bow. See illustration 223 of Buchner's *Musical Instruments through the Ages*. Diagram 80 is a sketch of the instrument. A similar instrument is shown in diagram 216 of *Stringed Instruments of the Middle Ages* by Hortense Panum.

Because of the difficulties of intonation and the kind of tone produced, neither of these devices should be considered as a serious musical instrument but they are good fun to make. Both show how the simplest of materials may be used to produce interesting sounds.

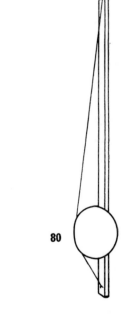

79

80

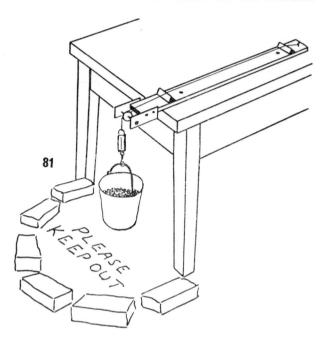

More precise experiments may be made by using the sonometer from the school laboratory. If this apparatus is not available a simple substitute may be made. Cut a flat board $30'' \times 3'' \times 1''$ from strong, dry timber. Part of an old shelf will serve the purpose. Synthetic board should be avoided because of its lack of longitudinal strength. A pulley will be needed for the wire to pass over and thus change the pull from vertical to horizontal; this pulley could be from an old sash window or from a clothes airer. A short shaft of steel about $\frac{1}{4}''$ in diameter and two wooden cheeks about $10'' \times 2'' \times \frac{1}{2}''$ will complete the mechanical assembly. Triangular-section wood will form loose bridges. Screw the cheeks to the board so that the wire leaves the pulley horizontally at a height of about $\frac{1}{4}''$ below the bridge height. This will ensure that the bridges isolate the length of string one wishes to deal with, i.e. $25\frac{5}{8}''$ to begin with. Diagrams 81 and 82 show the general arrangement.

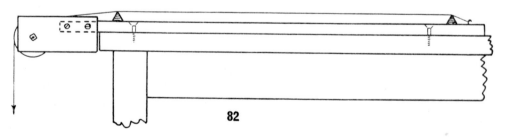

Use a small bucket to hold the sand which is needed to provide the tension on the wire and arrange in between bucket and wire a tension spring balance to weigh to 25 lb. This will enable the weights to be noted as they change. Everything must be made safe. There are three important safety precautions:

a. The board must be screwed or cramped to the top of a table or low cupboard so that the weight of the bucket and sand cannot overturn the apparatus.

b. A safety barrier, e.g. of bricks, must be placed around the space where the bucket would fall if the wire broke; no pupil should set foot inside this barrier.

c. The wire must be *music wire* and not commercial wire from the ironmonger. Reasonable weights must be used to put this wire in tension. The thinner, uncovered plectrum guitar strings are recommended for this work because it is known what sounding lengths they should be given and what notes they should give at these lengths. The weights can be given accordingly.

An instrument, e.g. a piano or guitar, should be available for pitch comparisons during these tests. Use at first a no. 2 plectrum guitar string on the sonometer and suspend from the end a combined weight (bucket and sand) of about $4\frac{1}{4}$ lb. This tension should give the note B, an octave below the nominal pitch of the string when the sounding length is $25\frac{5}{8}''$.

1. Compare the notes given by (a) bowing the string with a violin bow, (b) plucking the string, and (c) striking gently with a pencil. Have the three notes the same pitch?

2. Compare the *quality* of the notes given by bowing, plucking and striking when the point of attack is varied. Can differences be heard within each group? Describe any differences you hear.

83

notes mentioned in the sonometer experiments

3. Move one of the bridges to the midway point. What note does the half-length string give? Remember that the tension is the same.

4. Return the bridge to its original position and slowly add sand to the bucket. Pluck the string as the sand is added. What happens to the pitch of the note? Keep adding sand until the string note has risen an octave to b. What is now the

75

weight of sand and bucket? Express this new weight as a ratio to the original weight.

5. Take off the bucket and fit a no. 1 plectrum guitar string in place of the no. 2 string. Replace the bucket. What weight is needed to tension this string to the B given by the first weight hung on the no. 2 string? Add sand until the note reaches the b and record this weight also. Why should these weights be less than those needed for the no. 2 string?

6. Repeat experiment no. 4 with the no. 1 string, taking e and e' as the notes to be checked. Do results tally with those from experiment no. 4?

7. Look up Mersenne's laws, which were recorded in 1636. Find out also how much of this work had already been studied by Pythagoras and by Galileo.

8. Leave in the bucket the weight needed for the note e'. Place in the middle of the string a small vee piece of paper as a *rider*. Tweezers will be needed. Rest a lyre on the baseboard of the apparatus and pluck the same note e' on this instrument. Watch the behaviour of the rider. Pluck also the notes d' and f'$^\sharp$ on the lyre, still resting the instrument on the board. Does the rider move in response to these notes? Pluck the note e an octave below and take note of any movement of the rider.

Knowledge of some of these characteristics is utilised in making musical instruments. The bass strings on the harp and pianoforte, for instance, may be made thicker and heavier instead of longer. Instruments much longer than those in use today would otherwise be needed to accommodate the very long strings.

Other examples are:

a. The violin with four strings of the same length but with the top and bottom strings tuned to an interval of nearly two octaves.

b. The guitar with six strings of the same length, these separated by intervals which total two octaves. Careful choice of string thickness has made it possible for the guitar frets to be placed at right angles to the strings. This allows identical intervals to be stopped from each string by pressing the fingers behind the frets.

CLASSIFICATION OF INSTRUMENTS USING STRINGS. Lists and pictures of musical instruments should be collected. Hearing some of the instruments played will add to the knowledge gained. This might be a long-term project which involved reading, drawing and listening to radio and recordings.

HEADINGS suggested for classification. It is not suggested that all these classi-fications should be investigated at once.

a String instruments of today's orchestra (strictly 'strings')
b The instruments of the string quartet
c The instruments of the piano quartet
d Instruments which have both keyboard and strings
e String instruments that have flat backs
f String instruments that have flat bellies
g String instruments that have curved backs
h String instruments that have curved bellies
i String instruments that have soundposts
j String instruments that have no soundposts
k String instruments that are bowed
l Instruments with strings that are plucked by hand or by plectrum
m Instruments with strings that are plucked mechanically
n Instruments with strings that are struck in some way
o String instruments that are mentioned in the Bible
p String instruments that are mentioned by Shakespeare
q Instruments which have sympathetic strings.

Visits to museums might be made and also to churches where carvings and stained glass illustrate instruments of music. As many actual examples as possible should be borrowed or demonstrated by good players. Recordings of string combinations should be heard, preferably on the day when the actual instruments are on show.

Sound from moving air

Tubes of many kinds make notes when they are blown across the ends. Rim-blown flutes have been used in many parts of the world. The syrinx or Pan-pipes is a bundle of short lengths of tubing bound together in the shape of a raft. In this country boys used to make elder twigs and cow-parsley stems into simple whistles and flageolets. (Care should be taken, if this idea is followed, not to use the stems of the hemlock because these are poisonous. This plant resembles cow parsley.) Short pieces of stem may be bound together for Pan-pipes and, with care, simple whistles may be made. The offcuts of the tubular glockenspiel may also be made into Pan-pipes. Short lengths of $\frac{1}{2}''$ diameter pipe may be stopped at one end and bound together. Plasticine or softwood plugs should be pressed

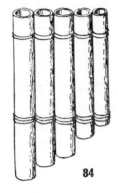

84

into the ends of the tubing and the notes tuned by pushing in the plugs further or by withdrawing them slightly. Five pieces would make a pentatonic scale and for a boy provide quite a challenge in assembly and tuning.

Bamboo offcuts are useful. Some pieces should have the nodal closures left intact and some may be closed with corks. Bamboo is usually too big to be tied into Pan-pipe assemblies but the tuned pieces may be used as handbells are sometimes used, one piece to each child. Because the pieces are not actually held in the mouth, the hygiene hazard is not great.

1. Sort out a scale from the pieces and put the notes in tune by shortening the pipes.

2. Notice if the scale is in order of length of pipe.

3. Try to decide what makes some notes easier to play than others.

4. Play a tune as with handbells, one pipe to each pupil.

An elementary transverse flute may be made from a piece of bamboo which has at one end a natural nodal closure. A suitable size of pipe would be 10″ long and $\frac{5}{8}$″ bore. Drill a $\frac{3}{16}$″ hole in the wall of the pipe about 1″ from the node and enlarge it with a knife or file until a note may be sounded by blowing across the hole. Fingerholes may be bored along the pipe to produce a sequence of notes. For more detailed information about pipe-making in general one should consult *Making and Playing Bamboo Pipes*, published by The Dryad Press.

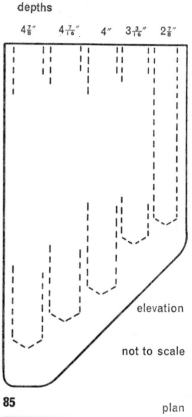

depths

$4\frac{7}{8}$″ $4\frac{7}{16}$″ 4″ $3\frac{3}{16}$″ $2\frac{7}{8}$″

elevation

not to scale

85   plan

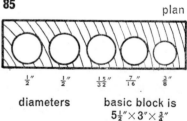

diameters

$\frac{1}{2}$″ $\frac{1}{2}$″ $\frac{15}{32}$″ $\frac{7}{16}$″ $\frac{3}{8}$″

basic block is
$5\frac{1}{2}$″ × 3″ × $\frac{3}{4}$″

PAN-PIPES may be made from a block of hardwood or from plastic material. If a pillar drill is available, accurately-spaced holes should be drilled in the block and tuned to a scale. Diagram 85 gives the approximate sizes. Long-reach drills may be needed for this work; the usual jobbers' length drills may be too short. Suitable woods are sycamore, pear, box and Honduras rosewood. If sycamore is used, the block should first be soaked in molten paraffin wax and allowed to cool before the drilling is done. The other woods should be treated with raw linseed oil after the drilling. Both these treatments help to seal the grain against the penetration of moisture from the breath. If any hole is drilled too deeply, its note may be sharpened by tamping into the hole a small piece of Plasticine to reduce the sounding length. Holes should run parallel with the grain of the wood.

CLASSIFICATION OF INSTRUMENTS which need moving air to produce sound. Pictures and diagrams should be collected.
- *a*   Wind instruments of the orchestra
- *b*   Brass band instruments
- *c*   Military band instruments
- *d*   Instruments which have fingerholes
- *e*   Instruments which have keyboards
- *f*   Reed instruments or pipes; single reed, double reed, metal reed
- *g*   Closed or open pipes and types of bore, e.g. parallel, taper
- *h*   Wind instruments mentioned in the Bible and by Shakespeare.

Borrow or demonstrate as many instruments as possible and try to make arrangements with the clergyman and organist to visit a church or chapel to examine the organ. The different sections of the organ should be shown and heard. Drawings of the lay-out should be made and lists of the stops. Finding some of the origins of the names would be an interesting search.

A diapason or a flute organ pipe might be made in the workshop. Reference should be made to books on organs or books on the physics of sound.

Sound from rods and bars

Offcuts of wood or even chopped firewood sticks will give notes when the pieces are laid on a foam plastic mat and struck with a small beater. Sorting a collection of odd pieces into the semblance of a scale can be interesting. Lay each piece on a piece of foam bath mat and tap each in the middle with a beater. Try hard beaters and also felt ones and try to recognise the true note; there will be also from each a 'clang note' rather higher in pitch. Some people seem to hear this higher note more clearly than the true note. Decide which beater gives the best notes.

This exercise might be given to children to work through in turn; it would be a good opportunity for one to help another. The relation should be noted between length and cross-section of the pieces and the note, the kind of wood (whether hardwood or softwood) and the best striking point. Encourage the children to play tunes on these pieces.

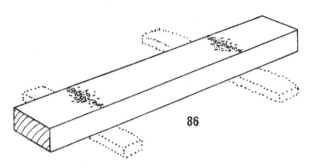

NODES ON A RIGID BAR. Take a tuned batten, preferably one with a flat upper surface, lay it quite level on a foam plastic bath mat and sprinkle the wood with fairly coarse sawdust. Tap the middle of the batten with a beater and watch the behaviour of the sawdust particles. These will begin to move and as the tapping continues, some particles will fall off. Other particles will travel slowly towards two distinct points where there will be eventually small collections of sawdust. At this stage try to localise these collections even more markedly by supporting the batten with ¾" strips of foam laid under the collecting points. A little more tapping will clear the ends and the middle of the batten of all sawdust. The restful state of the dust at two points suggests that, in spite of the fact that the wood is vibrating, there are two places where the wood is scarcely moving. These two points are *nodes*. Compare this batten with a string in tension; with the string, the ends must be fixed to allow tension to be applied and the ends must be classed as nodes; the ends of the batten are free to move and they evidently do move freely or the sawdust would not be shaken off. Such a rigid piece of wood appears to be too stiff to vibrate freely but the vibrations may be felt quite easily if one touches the wood lightly with fingertips as the beater is used.

In making a musical instrument such as a xylophone or glockenspiel, support for the battens should be as near as possible to the nodes where the damping effect of the padded frame will have least effect. It is necessary to tabulate the proportions into which the nodes divide the battens. Maximum movement and sound will thus be obtained when the frame is so shaped that each batten is supported at its nodal points. From the table of test figures from several battens may be calculated the proportions as percentages of the lengths and the frame size may be established from these figures.

Similar trials with the metal bars of a metallophone will confirm the results gained from the wooden battens. Interesting patterns of nodal lines may also be seen on other vibrating surfaces if the appropriate experiments of Chladni are carried out. This is advanced work and should not be undertaken lightly. Refer to *The Physics of Music* by Alexander Wood and published as a University Paperback by Methuen.

CLASSIFICATION OF PERCUSSION INSTRUMENTS. Names alone are insufficient. The aim should be to provide for each instrument named a drawing or photograph which gives a good idea of the size as well as the appearance.

- *a* Accepted percussion instruments of the orchestra
- *b* Additions to this group for special purposes
- *c* Percussion instruments which have keyboards
- *d* 'Solid' percussion e.g. xylophone, metallophone
- *e* 'Hollow' percussion e.g. drum, guiro, slit drum
- *f* Membrane percussion
- *g* Percussion from wood
- *h* Percussion from metal
- *i* Percussion instruments which have strings
- *j* Percussion instruments mentioned in the Bible and by Shakespeare.

Suppliers

Messrs. Mickleburgh of Stokes Croft, Bristol 1 have agreed to supply the special items needed for the string instruments. These are plectrum guitar strings (loop-ended), piano wire, short zither wrest pins and tuning keys.

Only specialist timber merchants will be able to supply jacaranda or palissander for the battens of the resonated xylophone. The last parcel of jacaranda battens was supplied to me by Bland and Tucker Ltd. of Chapel Street, Thornbury, Gloucestershire. Alternative timbers are suggested in the text of the book.

'Tonewood' has not been specified for any instrument but it is mentioned in chapter four. Tools and materials for the luthier may be obtained from Sydney Evans Ltd., 49 Berkley Street, Birmingham 1.

Glossary

arris: in this situation, the sharp edge formed by two smooth surfaces meeting at a right angle.

fell: literally a skin. On a drum this may be called the vellum, the head or the skin.

kerf: the narrow groove cut by a saw. Our word 'carve' has the same root.

knop: the head or knob of a drum stick.

lath: a thin, narrow piece of wood, not to be confused with lathe.

lapping: folding over the edges of a drum skin and attaching to a hoop.

lashing: the zig-zag cords on a drum for tensioning the head.

luthier: strictly a lute maker but now applies to a builder of violin, viola and cello.

m.s. mild steel.

mull: scrim.

scarf: a type of longitudinal mitre joint, usually in wood.

stop: to press a string with the finger against a fingerboard to shorten the sounding length of the string.

tacked drum: a drum on which the head is nailed or tacked in place.

tamp: to press down material into a hole.

vellum: skin, fell or head.

whip: to secure with several turns of fine thread; to bind; to serve.

Bibliography

1   Baines, A. *Catalogue of Musical Instruments* (Victoria and Albert Museum) Vol. II Non-key board H.M.S.O.

2   „   *European and American Musical Instruments* Batsford

3   „   *Musical Instruments through the Ages* Pelican

4   Barnard, E. *Playing with Sounds* Curwen Press

5   Britten, B. and Holst, I. *The Story of Music* Rathbone Books London

6   Blocksidge, K. M. *How to Use Melodic Percussion Instruments* Nursery Schools Association

7   Blocksidge, K. M. *Making Musical Apparatus and Instruments* University of London Press

8   Buchner, A. *Musical Instruments throughout the Ages* Spring Books

9   Donington, R. *The Instruments of Music* Methuen

10 Galloway, M. *Making and Playing Bamboo Pipes* Dryad Press

11 Galpin, F. W. *Old English Instruments of Music* (Revised Thurston Dart 1965) Methuen

12 Harrison and Rimmer *European Musical Instruments* Studio Vista

13 Horniman Museum Publication No. 3995 *Musical Instruments* London County Council, County Hall, s.e.1

14 Jahnel, F. *Die Gitarre und ihr Bau* (in German) Verlag Das Instrument

15 Jeans, Sir J. *Science and Music* Cambridge University Press

16 Kettelkamp, L. *Drums, Rattles and Bells* Wheaton

17 Mandell and Wood *Make Your Own Musical Instruments* Sterling Publishing Company, New York

18 Marcuse, S. *Musical Instruments; a comprehensive dictionary* Country Life

19 Panum, H. *Stringed Instruments of the Middle Ages* William Reeves

20 Price and Levine *Sounds All Around* Blackie

21 Sachs, C. *The History of Musical Instruments* Norton (Dent)

22 Western, W. G. *Sound* Oxford University Press

23 Williams, W. G. *Looking and Listening* J. Murray

24 Wood, A. *The Physics of Music* Methuen

Index

Other Craft Books
by Dryad

DRYAD PRESS
NORTHGATES · LEICESTER